MW00658100

Courageous School Leadership

Courageous School Leadership

Don't Let the Why Get Lost in the How

David C. Jeck

ROWMAN & LITTLEFIELD
Lanham • Boulder • New York • London

Published by Rowman & Littlefield
An imprint of The Rowman & Littlefield Publishing Group, Inc.
4501 Forbes Boulevard, Suite 200, Lanham, Maryland 20706
www.rowman.com

86-90 Paul Street, London EC2A 4NE

British Library Cataloguing in Publication Information Available

Library of Congress Cataloging-in-Publication Data

ISBN 978-1-4758-7043-5 (cloth) | 978-1-4758-7045-9 (epub)

♾™ The paper used in this publication meets the minimum requirements of American
National Standard for Information Sciences—Permanence of Paper for Printed Library
Materials, ANSI/NISO Z39.48-1992. ∼

This book is dedicated to two groups of people. The first includes any person who attended school always feeling like they were the dumbest kid in class and were, perhaps, even told as much. Anyone who ever rode the "little bus" and was bullied as a result. Anyone who sat in the back of the classroom praying that they would not be called on to answer a question, read a passage, or write something on the chalkboard. Anyone regularly pulled from the "regular" education classroom in order to receive services elsewhere. Those who used or use humor as a distraction or coping mechanism in order to avoid being embarrassed. Those called "retard" and often assigned the worst teachers because the "best" kids were often assigned the "best" teachers. Anyone who was excluded from playing games at recess because they were one of those kids in the "special" classroom. This book is for you.
The second group are those teachers and school leaders who witness all these things happening and do something about it. Teachers who see the beauty and potential in every kid, who understand and recognize the unique gift that every child possesses. Those exceptional teachers who insist on teaching the kids who need the best teacher the most. To school leaders who recognize that behavior issues might have something to do with a kid being hungry, neglected, sleep deprived, or even abused at home. Those school leaders who provide washing machines in their schools for kids who can't wash their clothes at home and those who have fought to end "meal shaming" in cafeterias and who make sure that needy kids have access to a backpack full of food to take home every Friday afternoon. This book is for you also. You are a blessing.
If you or a close family member were part of the first group and experienced that sort of treatment, the emotional bruises have perhaps

never healed entirely. No doubt, things have changed positively and dramatically for special needs kids, kids in poverty, and kids of color. There is no doubt that our attitudes, processes, and resources have all improved significantly, but we still have a long way to go.
The second group is one that we should all belong to.
School staff who are willing to stand up for kids in need and let them know that they care about them are our nation's most important resource.

Contents

Foreword

In *Courageous School Leadership: Don't Let the Why Get Lost in the How*, David Jeck provides us with a practical and insightful guide on the challenges facing educational leaders. This refreshing new book comes at a critical moment. Throughout the United States, educational leaders find themselves increasingly under scrutiny and sometimes under direct personal attack. Regardless of this pressure, they have to find a way to make what are sometimes tough decisions that will invariably piss some people off.

Drawing on his many years of experience as a superintendent and educator, Jeck offers practical wisdom on how to think through complex educational issues and how to lead with clarity of vision, moral integrity, and a strong dose of humor. Having seen Jeck and dozens of other leaders like him handle the turmoil that often accompanies controversial educational issues, I cannot overstate the value of his insights.

Regardless of the nature of the challenge—whether it's financial, and tough choices have to be made over what to cut from a budget that's already been squeezed; social, involving the need to find a way to ensure that all students, regardless of racial or socioeconomic backgrounds, receive a quality education; or health related, such as controversies over mask-wearing and vaccines—educational leaders must find ways to make sound decisions. They must be able to listen to the concerns of parents who may be preoccupied with the interests of their children but less aware of or concerned about the interests of other children. They must be responsive to the concerns of employees whose demands may not be well aligned with the best interests of children. And they must listen to and take the heat from strident critics without crumbling or taking those attacks personally.

Jeck provides insights on how to do all of this, and he does so with the kind of practical wisdom that educational leaders will appreciate. In fact, anyone who has held a leadership role in a company, nonprofit, college, or family, and anyone who is interested in understanding the challenges faced by schools today will find this book to be an eye-opener and a valuable resource.

I've seen Jeck in action, so I know that his words have been matched by his efforts. This is why *Courageous School Leadership: Don't Let the Why Get Lost in the How* is much more than another education leadership book. It is a practical guide on how to make a difference and have a positive impact on the world through education. It comes to us at a critical time.

—Dr. Pedro Noguera, author, speaker, educator, and dean of the University of Southern California's Rossier School of Education

Preface

As I neared the completion of this book, my oldest son David asked me several times if he could read it. I kept telling him to wait a bit and I'd give him a more complete draft to review once it was better organized and edited. I wanted David to like what he read because his opinion meant so much to me, and because he exemplified so much of what is contained in it: the importance of kindness, acceptance, understanding, courage, and humility. He took very seriously the premise that we belong to each other, and it is our duty to care for each other. David clung so tightly to these beliefs, and my youngest son, Caleb, has followed so closely in his brother's footsteps. They are my heroes.

A short story about my beautiful son . . .

If I am safely able to do so, I give money to the souls standing at intersections and corners asking for charity. I do it often because I take literally the mantra that we all belong to each other. We are to care for each other. Yes, I understand that these people might use the money to buy something they shouldn't, but perhaps they *are* hungry. Perhaps they *do* need some gas for their car. Perhaps they *are* out of work and desperate for help. It's not my place to judge; it's my responsibility to help those who need help.

My son and I met at a fast-food restaurant for lunch, about halfway between our two homes. After lunch, we pulled out of the parking lot at about the same time in our different cars. He and I were both in the far right lane, and three lanes over to the left was a man holding a sign, asking for money. My son, God bless him, made a sharp left turn, cut across three lanes (there was no other traffic), and gave the guy some money. Fortunately, no police were there to witness it, but I did, and *proud* can't begin to describe how I felt.

David passed away unexpectedly on December 6, 2021, just prior to the completion of this book. He was just twenty-eight years old. I figured we had plenty of time together, so I was in no rush to share a draft with him. I regret that, but as I review what I have written, I see David in it and draw close to him. David would have grinned broadly at the references to him in this book. He had a big, beautiful smile that made everyone around him smile also. I miss him so much. The hurt will never go away, but we are comforted by the fact that he influenced so many people in such a positive way.

Figure P.1. David Collins Jeck

Introduction

When you have exhausted all possibilities, remember this—you haven't.

—Thomas Edison

There is an old story about Abraham Lincoln told many years ago that serves as a guidepost for anyone hoping to influence others. The message—historically accurate or not—is simple yet profound, just like our sixteenth president. Lincoln was a regular churchgoer, but his religious views are a bit of a mystery. He never joined a church, and he was by all accounts a skeptic when it came to organized religion. Although his references to God were frequent, and he had a deep and thorough understanding of the scriptures, he was also quick to point out hypocrisy in the church and among "Christian" politicians.

While president, he preferred to attend a church with his family that was close to the White House, but he sometimes attended evening services alone. He would enter quietly after the service had begun and then slip out before it ended. On one occasion, as he departed from an evening service, he was joined by a man who invited himself to walk with Lincoln. As they walked toward the White House, the man asked the president what he thought of the sermon. Lincoln said, "It was indeed a very good message," but he expressed disappointment because the preacher had not "told us what to do with it."

It wouldn't make sense to write a book intended to help people unless it also included direction about what to do with the book's information. We are all bombarded with "stuff" we need to read, consider, and respond to with action. The barrage is daily and relentless, but we do it anyway because we supposedly have to. The goal ought to be to provide readers with some things they can actively incorporate and reflect on, things that, perhaps, will make them more effective leaders.

What K–12 public education needs now more than ever are courageous, confident, and outspoken leaders who stand on principle and marginalize the self-absorbed people who get in the way, simply because they have no interest in helping all kids be successful. These folks seem to be everywhere.

Over the past few years, school leaders have been back on their heels, on the defensive, fearful of taking the kinds of stands that might make life more difficult for them, stands that typically involve making decisions that are in the best interest of kids. It's not fair to blame any of them. These have been excruciatingly difficult times, and all school leaders have been challenged in ways that they could not have imagined.

This book is intended to address the "fear" problem while offering solutions, filling toolboxes, encouraging the discouraged, and inspiring those who, perhaps, don't believe that their skill sets mirror the long-held assumptions about what school leaders ought to be like. Those current and future leaders who do not fit the traditional leadership model, who hated and consistently experienced failure when they were in school, perhaps have an advantage, the advantage of knowing why some kids struggle, why providing equity for kids is critically important, and why courageous leadership has never been more important.

If any of this resonates with you, stop for a moment and consider your "why." Why do you do what you do? What is driving you? Why did you pick up this book? Lincoln was right for admonishing the minister for not providing more direction, but Lincoln was most certainly someone who understood exactly what his why was. Do you know what yours is, and does it come before your how?

REFLECT/CONNECT

At the end of each chapter, there is an opportunity for you to reflect and connect.

Reflect: Pause to consider and/or take a suggested courageous action.
Connect: Share your reflections and experiences with a community of courageous leaders just like you by using social media.

SECTION ONE

Pilotage

Perhaps this section should have been titled "Educational Leadership," but "pilotage" sounds more technical and cooler. Piloting implies that, within the realm of leadership, there are risks being taken and new paths being explored. That is what educational leadership should be about.

Chapter 1

Turkeys and Eagles

It's not just what you know, but how you practice what you know that determines how well the learning serves you later.

—Peter C. Brown

Once upon a time, a group of turkeys gathered together and were lamenting the fact that they could not fly. They were discouraged at seeing no way to overcome this savagely unfair reality. They were birds, after all, so how could this be? Then one of the turkeys who fancied himself the leader of the flock, spoke up: "I've got it! Let's hire some eagles to teach us how to fly. They are the best flyers around!" So the lead turkey hired some eagles to teach them how to fly.

On the appointed morning, all the turkeys arrived at a large barn filled with round tables, each with a small pile of candy in the center, sticky notes, and markers. Toward the edges of the barn, beside easels, large poster paper, a projector, and a screen, stood three very confident and good-looking eagles.

The training—we'll call it Turkey Development Training—began with a lecture called Introduction to Flight. The turkeys took notes feverishly. Then the eagles showed a video detailing the many different types of flying. A guest speaker shared with the turkeys how she had overcome her insecurities and learned to fly. She promised the turkeys they could too. The turkeys were very excited.

After lunch, the eagles began to teach each turkey to fly. Gradually, the turkeys began to fly short distances, albeit clumsily. Then they flew a bit more, and a bit more, and even a bit more. By the end of the day, all the turkeys were flying in and around the rafters, showing off their newly developed skill. The turkeys were very happy and very confident.

The eagles then asked the turkeys to complete an evaluation form, and then they opened the doors to the barn. All the turkeys walked home.

3

All our great ideas, new initiatives, exciting programs, and guest speakers will not move the achievement needle one bit if our teachers don't buy what we are selling. You can teach a turkey how to fly, but the turkey won't apply the skill outside of the in-service if they don't buy into the need for the skill or understand why it matters. Trying to improve our instructional models without getting buy-in from stakeholders is futile.

In education, we've seen the pattern play out over and over again: new software, devices, curriculums, makerspaces, sensory rooms, project-based learning, and so on don't take any of us to a new place unless we follow a very simple model built around common strategies familiar to us, strategies that ensure buy-in. Books have been written about these strategies. Speakers have made careers out of promoting these strategies. They are:

Build Trust: Do what you say you're going to do. Be visible. Listen more than you talk. Smile. Support and defend your people. Always tell the truth. When you make a mistake, admit it and move on.

Observe: Take walks in your building(s) regularly and leave the evaluation hat in your office. What are the kids doing? Focus on their level of engagement. Be willing to confront the stuff that you don't like.

Investigate: What are the true needs of your school and/or school community? These needs may simply require improved relationships, not necessarily the need for a new program or product that may end up on the shelf in a couple of years.

Collaborate and Listen (with and to Everyone): Collaboration is energetic communication—not just talking. Genuine listening occurs when your goal is to understand and generate questions. Combine the two—collaboration and listening—and you've got healthy, meaningful, and trust-building dialogue.

Measure: Is the new product/strategy making any difference? Vendors are typically nice people, but they *are all* trying to sell the silver bullet, the solution to all of your problems, the easy fix. But these things do not exist. Vendor products may *help.* They may make your life easier. But they are never going to be more than one piece of a very large puzzle.

Although it is difficult to measure emotional growth, problem-solving skills, resilience, and the ability to work with others, it doesn't mean we can't. We monitor what we value, and these are the skills that we have thus far not measured with fidelity.

Hold People Accountable: As you hold people accountable, always remember that others are watching. If they see that you are willing to help someone be a better educator by expecting results from them, even if holding the person accountable is very uncomfortable for the both of you, those observing others are being motivated too.

Recognize and Reward Your People: When it comes to recognition and reward, a little goes a long way. It will go even further if recognition and reward are accompanied by consistency, sincerity, and a bit of enthusiasm. People can sniff out insincerity pretty quickly—if they feel that you are simply checking a box, you'll become the butt of many jokes.

Finally, constantly remind yourself that nothing is ever going to replace the importance of the relationship between teacher and student. Nothing. This is a truism repeated several times in this book. What happens in the classroom each day, between teacher and students, is always going to be the most influential dynamic within the gigantic world of education. Don't fool yourself into believing that you have some kind of magical influence because of your intellect, ideas, authority, or magnetism. Everything begins and ends with the teachers and the students. Your job is to help them learn to fly, fly better, and keep flying, even after the barn door opens.

REFLECT/CONNECT

Reflect: Your job is to help them learn to fly, fly better, and keep flying, even after the barn door opens. What can you do to ensure that professional development is actually applied and is tailored to the needs of your staff? How can you make it stick?

Connect: Share your reflections and experiences with a community of courageous leaders just like you by using social media.

Chapter 2

The Stuff They Don't Tell You

There are known knowns. These are things we know that we know. There are known unknowns. That is to say, there are things that we know we don't know. But there are also unknown unknowns. There are things we don't know we don't know.

—Donald Rumsfeld

When the debate is lost, slander becomes
the tool of the loser.

—Anonymous

Why do we teachers and school administrators not share with our colleagues what is needed in order to lead? Some teachers and administrators have never led, so they may not know what to do. *Some* administrators find the work too hard or aren't very good at it, so they sometimes become higher educators.

Nothing against the people who induct new or aspiring administrators, but it seems that few higher-level educators actually have meaningful experience doing what we do in schools each day. They just don't, so they really can't accurately prepare you for what to expect. This is not to say that what they pass along to students isn't valuable and helpful—it typically is. It's just that they aren't going to be able to describe accurately what your life will be like, what "one-off" challenges you'll face, and what impact it all will have on your mental health.

There is a vast difference between theory and practice. This book leans heavily toward the importance of practice. As part of most any administrative induction program, most if not all are required to take a course called "The Principalship," or something similar. Hopefully, if you have or will take this course, it will taught by someone with significant and successful experience

7

as a school leader, but even if that is the case, there will still be many holes to fill upon completion. Becoming a school principal or superintendent is like getting married: you're never really ready for it, but you do it anyway.

1. Here's what they *don't* tell you: Don't be surprised when people—other than your mom, your spouse, and some of the folks you work closely with—don't seem to care about the trials you are experiencing. You will have bad days and deal with some really stressful stuff in your personal life—marital issues, financial concerns, problems with your own children—on top of what is happening at school. For the most part, people don't care.

If you've ever shared details with stakeholders of your own personal struggles, you'll relate. It's sort of like trying to provide parenting advice: it's generally not well-received. Don't expect sympathy or compassion from anyone other than the folks who love and care about you. To the others, you are a leader who can take whatever is dished out without reacting. If you do react, you'll be the story, and you don't want that. This isolation is one of the most difficult aspects of leadership, but it does not preclude any of us from truly caring and trying to help those who desperately need it. This is why we do what we do.

2. Mental health issues are real. School leaders interact with dozens, hundreds, thousands of people, countless numbers from all walks of life. Some of these people will have mental health issues, some diagnosed and some not. Our dilemma is that we have to work with *all* of them, regardless. We must treat them all with the same level of concern and empathy. In the end, there may not be much that you can do for them, but it is your job to address their needs as best you know how.
3. Leave it at the office. Seriously: leave it at the office. The best you is the one who is rested, positive, and clear-minded. The leader who brings home the laptop each day, who answers and sends emails and texts no matter the day or hour, who can't let go of the day's stressors, and so on has fallen into a cycle that is difficult to break.

Once your parents, school board members, teachers, and colleagues know that you will engage with them 24-7, they will continue to invade your private world and will expect timely responses. Always being available will not make you a better leader, more effective, or a better human being. It will make you resent your job and some of the folks you work with and for. A really shitty email sent to you on Friday evening can wreck your entire weekend and your sacred time with your family—and it *is* sacred. Don't bring work home. Don't let it impact your relationships at home. Don't allow your home to become a second workplace

4. Be careful with self-medicating. As personal as this may seem, we need to talk about it. School leaders, especially superintendents, sometimes drink too much. This is not an attempt to paint every school leader with the same brush, but it is a problem, and every school leader ought to keep their guard up and avoid unhealthy habits.

The habit of self-medicating via alcohol may seem temporarily helpful, but it's tough on family, personal relationships, and health. It's an easy cycle to fall into. Don't be afraid or reluctant to see your doctor or a therapist and share your struggles. Taking a low dose, nonaddictive medication can be very helpful. We are all facing battles in our personal and professional lives that others know nothing about. Take care of yourself first and you'll be in a much better place to help others. The right medication can prevent you from waking up in the middle of the night with your brain going one hundred miles per hour with no relief in sight. If you think you need help, talk to your doctor.

5. Master the art of brevity when communicating via email. Better yet, make a call instead. If someone is upset and sends you an email with ten questions and you answer all of them, the next email you receive will have twenty questions. Don't try to win arguments and be persuasive via email. It's a waste of time and energy. Just call or respond with one of my favorites: "Thank you for your email. I will consider what you have written and respond if necessary." If I am feeling a bit saucy, I'll send this one: "Thank you for your email. I'll give it the consideration it deserves."

Engaging with people via email and trying to win them over has about a 5 percent success rate. It's like Bill Murray once said: "It's hard to win an argument with a smart person, but it's damn near impossible to win an argument with a stupid person."

6. Don't take any of it personally, even if it's meant to be personal. People are never going to understand what each day of your professional life is like—they never will, so always assume that they don't. For many of the people who attack you, you are nothing more than a big, emotionless target, someone who is supposed to be able to take it. To some extent they are right. School leadership requires a thick skin and short memory.
7. Don't take yourself too seriously, but take your work very seriously. What we do impacts many people in a profound way. It's easy to get caught up in the drama, and every day has drama, but understand that

everyone is looking at you. How will you respond? Will your mood suddenly change? Will your hair suddenly catch on fire because someone else's is ablaze? As a colleague once shared, "Everyone is looking at the big dog. They want to see how you will react during the worst of times. Don't let them down!"

8. Know when to disengage. This is a very, very difficult goal for those of us who pride ourselves in our ability to communicate effectively, fix problems, offer solutions, talk folks off the ledge, deescalate situations, and so on. Sometimes, in spite of our best efforts, we fail to do any of these things. Sometimes we have to take the steps that run contrary to what we believe as leaders, and those steps are to walk away from the people and situations we cannot help.

Frankly, some people calling or emailing looking for help really don't want it anyway; they simply take pleasure in occupying space in your mind rent-free and enjoy having a good story to share on social media. Sometimes it is okay to walk away. Let those people who don't want help call the superintendent, school board member, board of supervisor member, their attorney, the governor. If you have exhausted every strategy you know, let them pound sand for a while.

9. Don't tolerate verbal abuse and threats. This point relates closely to number 8. When the abuse starts, simply let the offender know that you aren't going to tolerate it and that your staff does not have to tolerate it either. It is okay to insist that you and your staff be treated with the same courtesy and respect that you show. Remember the words of Miss Manners: "When people start hurling insults at you, you know their minds are closed and there's no point in debating. You disengage yourself as quickly as possible from the situation."

Our Burden

The amount of responsibility we've added to the plates of public school educators would be criminal in any other industry. The outstanding and revealing work of Jamie Vollmer clearly demonstrates the immense burden on K–12 educators. His work is an eye-opener for anyone critical of public education or for those who simply don't understand what all our fuss is about. The fact is, public schools are getting crushed under the weight of expectations that have no connection to simply teaching kids the skills they need in order to communicate, problem solve, and synthesize sometimes disconnected information.

In his article "The Increasing Burden Placed on America's Public Schools," Vollmer carefully lists all the tasks gradually heaped upon schools since the beginning of public education in 1640 in the United States. Vollmer explains that schools were tasked by the Puritans with teaching "basic reading, some writing, and arithmetic skills" and cultivating "values that serve a democratic society."

In the years since, *eighty-six* more responsibilities—ranging from physical education to typing classes to drug and alcohol abuse education to personal financial literacy to school lunch programs—have been dumped on schools. Jamie Vollmer (2012) created this long list, but it is important to share it in its entirety.

America's public schools can be traced back to the year 1640. The Massachusetts Puritans established schools to: 1) teach basic reading and some writing and arithmetic skills, and 2) cultivate values that serve a democratic society (some history and civics implied).

At the beginning of the twentieth century, however, politicians, academics, members of the clergy, and business leaders saw public schools as a logical site for the assimilation of immigrants and the social engineering of the citizens—and workers—of the new industrial age. They began to expand the curriculum and assign additional duties. That trend has accelerated ever since.

From 1900 to 1910, we shifted to our public schools' responsibilities related to

- nutrition
- immunization
- health (activities in the health arena multiply every year)

From 1910 to 1930, we added

- physical education (including organized athletics)
- practical arts/domestic science/home economics (including sewing and cooking)
- vocational education (including industrial and agricultural education)
- mandated school transportation

In the 1940s, we added

- business education (including typing, shorthand, and bookkeeping)
- art and music
- speech and drama
- half-day kindergarten

- school lunch programs (we take it for granted today, but the shift to school lunch programs was a huge step in feeding America's children one-third of their daily meals)

In the 1950s, we added

- expanded science and math education
- safety education
- driver's education
- expanded music and art education
- stronger foreign language requirements
- sex education (topics continue to escalate)

In the 1960s, we added

- Advanced Placement programs
- Head Start
- Title I
- adult education
- consumer education (purchasing resources, rights and responsibilities)
- career education (occupational options, entry-level skill requirements)
- peace, leisure, and recreation education (loved those sixties)

In the 1970s, the breakup of the American family accelerated, and we added

- drug and alcohol abuse education
- parenting education (techniques and tools for healthy parenting)
- behavior adjustment classes (including classroom and communication skills)
- character education
- special education (mandated by federal government)
- Title IX programs (greatly expanded athletic programs for girls)
- environmental education
- women's studies
- African American heritage education
- school breakfast programs (Today, some schools feed America's children two-thirds of their daily meals throughout the school year and all summer. Sadly, these are the only decent meals some children receive.)

In the 1980s, the floodgates opened, and we added

- keyboarding and computer education

- global education
- multicultural/ethnic education
- nonsexist education
- English as a second language and bilingual education
- teen pregnancy awareness
- Hispanic heritage education
- early childhood education
- Jump Start, Early Start, Even Start, and Prime Start
- full-day kindergarten
- preschool programs for children at risk
- after-school programs for children of working parents
- alternative education in all its forms
- stranger danger education
- antismoking education
- sexual abuse prevention education
- expanded health and psychological services
- child abuse monitoring (a legal requirement for all teachers)

In the 1990s, we added

- conflict resolution and peer mediation
- HIV/AIDS education
- CPR training
- death education
- America 2000 initiatives (Republican)
- inclusion
- expanded computer and internet education
- distance learning
- Tech Prep and School to Work programs
- technical adequacy
- assessment
- Postsecondary enrollment options
- concurrent enrollment options
- Goals 2000 initiatives (Democrat)
- expanded talented and gifted opportunities
- at risk and dropout prevention
- homeless education (including causes and effects on children)
- gang education (urban centers)
- service learning
- bus safety, bicycle safety, gun safety, and water safety education

In the first decade of the twenty-first century, we have added

- No Child Left Behind (Republican)
- bully prevention
- Antiharassment policies (gender, race, religion, or national origin)
- expanded early childcare and wraparound programs
- elevator and escalator safety instruction
- Body mass index evaluation (obesity monitoring)
- organ donor education and awareness programs
- personal financial literacy
- entrepreneurial and innovation skills development
- media literacy development
- contextual learning skill development
- health and wellness programs
- Race to the Top (Democrat)

Vollmer specifies that his list (which he invites teachers and administrators to add to) does not include standardized testing or any related activities (like test prep) or federal reporting requirements.

These are all really good things, important things, necessary things—but the list keeps growing. There seems to be no end in sight, and there will be none unless we stand up for ourselves and remind our stakeholders what our primary responsibilities are. Schools can't do it all, nor should they be asked to.

Vollmer's work should be broadcast, with a loudspeaker, across the nation. There is simply too much required of our schools, but we school employees shoulder some of the blame because we've allowed it to happen without much struggle. It's no wonder so many in our profession burn out, become frustrated, and ultimately leave. It's too much, and schools have become the last remaining dumping ground for all of those problems that society does not have a ready solution for. People place the burden on the schools and use the fact that public education is "taxpayer funded" as the rationalization for asking the impossible.

A glaring and somewhat startling recent example of the burden imposed on schools was our nation's response to the COVID-19 pandemic. School grounds hosted the "laboratories" and the "first responders" necessary for getting back to normal as quickly as possible. Our nation used the most vulnerable of our population as guinea pigs, opening schools as soon as possible, getting kids back in buildings while hundreds of thousands were dying.

Schools were then asked and/or required to become vaccination centers. Again, we are happy and willing to help whenever and wherever we can, but we are educators first. It never hurts to remind our communities exactly what we are here for and what obstacles prevent us from being the best versions of ourselves.

Reflect/Connect

Reflect: Knock it out of the park when in the office but pump the brakes at home. Identify three ways you can disengage from your job when you leave work, protect your time with your family, and preserve your own sanity.

Stay positive, knowing that your contribution is more than enough!

Connect: Share your reflections and experiences with a community of courageous leaders on social media.

Chapter 3

Choose the Right Path

And sorry I could not travel both.
And be one traveler, long I stood.

—Robert Frost, "The Road Less Traveled"

Frost's beautifully crafted imagery of an individual making a choice while standing at a fork in the road is somewhat chilling. Which path should the person take? The correct path seems obvious ("Because it was grassy and wanted wear"), but the speaker chooses the more difficult route. Why? Why choose the road less traveled by? Why not choose the easier, more attractive path?

Do you remember Colonel Frank Slade? He was played by Al Pacino in the film *The Scent of a Woman*. At the conclusion of the movie, Slade reflected, painfully, about the choices he had made in his own life. This is how he chose which road to take: "I have come to the crossroads of my life and I always knew the right path, without question I knew, but I never took it. You know why? Because it was too damn hard!"

What a tragedy.

There is nothing to be gained by choosing the easier path. Nothing. Avoiding the hard stuff as adults is just as bad as teaching our kids how to find and take the shortcuts. It is an easier way to go, but there is nothing to be gained.

In just a few words, Colonel Slade provides a concise summary of the issues we all face. Doing the right thing, making the right choice, heading in the right direction are hard.

Many of us share this advice with our children, and we remind ourselves even more often. We fail. We make the wrong choices. We take the easiest path at times but, as Colonel Slade said, we typically know the right path, especially when it comes to making choices about students.

17

As you probably have already experienced, it is not easy to make decisions always in the best interest of students. Many school leaders choose the easiest path because, well, it's easier. Choosing options that are in the best interest of kids in every situation is a hard way to lead. When we make these kinds of choices, the related adults sometimes become upset and feel underappreciated. They'll call their school board members. They'll complain in the teachers' lounge. Parents will hold court at the bus stop and, much worse, on social media.

Making a commitment to being a true student advocate is risky because so many of our folks are accustomed to just the opposite: decisions made in the best interest of themselves.

Some examples of choosing the right, but more difficult, path are as follows:

Daily bell scheduling: Does the daily bell schedule meet the needs of students or adults? Do students have an opportunity within the schedule to get some help from a teacher, grab a sausage biscuit, stretch their legs, etc.? There is a simple solution: carve out a fifteen-minute nutrition and "extra help" time after first block or period. If kids are hungry, they can eat, and if they need help, they can get it. Many of the adults in the building won't like it, but it's not for them, it's for the kids.

Criteria for admittance into honors/accelerated course: A somewhat controversial approach regarding parents who request that their child be placed in more challenging courses: give them a chance. It's up to the child to perform, but at least you are giving them a chance to perform at a higher level through a more challenging curriculum.

The outcry from your staff is predictable: "You are setting that child up for failure!" "You are watering down the course." "They haven't earned the opportunity." And . . . wait for it: "There isn't room in my classroom!" The fact is that many of these kids will be successful, especially when paired with an efficacious teacher, someone who believes in themselves and their kids. Such teachers are golden.

Some of the silliest excuses for not challenging nor providing opportunities for kids often come from some of the smartest people, completely arbitrary stuff like, "I only have room for twenty-six students because that is how many desks I have in my room," "We only offer one section of accelerated sixth grade math." Why? "Because that's how we've always done it." We should be asking this question: How many *could* be successful in an accelerated setting? The number you'll hear is probably greater than the number currently being served.

Don't let space or any other arbitrary factor determine which opportunities kids are provided. The easiest path for some is keeping the "top" kids together thereby maintaining a more comfortable and nonchallenging classroom environment.

But by choosing the more difficult as described in this example, kids will time and time again rise to the challenge we set for them as long as we believe in them and in our own ability to pull every kid up.

Student discipline system: Is the discipline system in your school or school division the more traditional "line them up and shoot them" model, or is it designed to teach proper behavior, reward good behavior, and build positive relationships between students and adult? Is it color-blind? Do you see trends wherein the Black kids are suspended a lot more than the White kids? It's okay to ask the question—someone needs to. Do you have teachers who send the Black and Brown kids to the office for being "disruptive," while the same behavior demonstrated by the White kids is chalked up to "getting the wiggles out?" Ask these questions. Confront these issues, even if doing so is hard.

Assessment and grading: if you're in education, you're familiar with the catastrophic impact of zeros:

Assignment One:	0
Assignment Two:	80
Assignment Three:	90
Assignment Four:	100
Average:	67.5 percent (a D or an F in some places)

Inexplicably, the debate over zeros continues. Unfortunately, too many educators simply won't let go of the practice of giving out zeros because they believe that it somehow teaches accountability. What it really teaches is absolutely nothing. It discourages and disenchants kids, but some school leaders won't rock this boat because they fear pushback. Take this advice: Rock this boat if you haven't already. Better yet, create a culture in your school wherein "not doing" is simply not acceptable.

Build into your schedule a time and place when and where kids *must* complete meaningful assignments. You can do this. if we as adults don't do our taxes, the IRS doesn't tell us that it's okay. Neither do they slap us with a zero. Instead, they require us to file, hounding us until we do. Expectations regarding *meaningful* schoolwork should be treated similarly.

When it comes to choosing the less-trodden, more challenging path, our collective experience demonstrates that choosing this path is the correct choice. Ultimately, the choice that will benefit students most directly.

Path Selections Tips

Many years ago, a former state superintendent-of-the-year in Virginia shared this piece of advice with a room full of aspiring school administrators: "Never touch the money and never accept from anyone anything that you can't eat." Practical and helpful advice.

Here are a few more favorite bits of wisdom:

- Return all phone calls within twenty-four hours.
- Do no favors. Choose the best person for the job.
- At the end of the day, you are the one who will be held accountable no matter if you were responsible or not.
- When you have to make a tough decision, look at a picture of your own kids and ask yourself how your decision will impact them.
- Don't pick fights with people who buy ink by the barrel.
- You can't fix crazy.
- The smartest person in the room *is* the entire room and everyone in it.
- If someone walks into your office with a monkey on their back trying to put that monkey on your back, make sure that when they leave your office the monkey is still on their back.

Here are a few not-so-good tips:

- Don't smile until Christmas: There are times in the classroom and in the office when we have to be stern, direct, and hold people accountable, but students want to know that you care about them and want what's best for them. When they see you smile and laugh along with them, poke fun at yourself, and act a little crazy at times. They will recognize your humanity and will respond to it positively.
- Treat them all the same: Or, better yet, treat them all like they're rich. If we are committed to providing equity for all kids, we can't treat them all the same. Some kids need more from us, or at least something different from us. Likewise, some kids need more independence and more freedom. *Equity* means giving kids what they need, when and how they need it, in order for them to achieve and grow to the fullest extent possible.
- Don't accept late work. You'll teach responsibility this way: We are facilitators of learning, not obstructers. "At-risk" kids need something different from us, and we have not been giving it to them systemically. What we have been doing up to this point has not helped them. We need to give them what they need.

If accepting late work means the kid has done the work and has experienced some degree of success, then why wouldn't we accept it? Start with the mantra that not doing is not acceptable, then work on the "on-time" piece.

REFLECT/CONNECT

Reflect: Identify one very difficult challenge that you have avoided because, well, it's very difficult. Identify it and set out to conquer it.

Doing the right thing, making the right choice, heading in the right direction are hard. What is one way you can advocate for kids that is difficult, even controversial, but clearly the right thing to do?

Connect: Share your reflections and experiences with a community of courageous leaders just like you by using social media.

Chapter 4

Listen—*Really* Listen

Most people do not listen with the intent to understand; they listen with the intent to reply.

—Stephen R. Covey

When you begin to worry, go find something to do. Get busy being a blessing to someone; do something fruitful. Talking about your problem or sitting alone, thinking about it, does no good; it serves only to make you miserable. Above all else, remember that worrying is totally useless. Worrying will not solve your problem.

—Joyce Meyer

We all know that guy who doesn't listen. He's the one who, while you are conversing with him, is visibly anxious to make his point and is certainly not listening to yours. You can tell by his body language, his impatience, and his inability to digest the points or information you are trying to convey.

How does this happen to people? Why are there so many bad listeners out there? Perhaps, as Covey states, they simply don't *want* to understand, they only want to reply.

Plenty has been written about what good listeners do, what active listening includes, and how to better convey to people that you are paying attention and are interested in what they are saying. It's an important skill. When people believe that they are being heard, they

- feel valued
- believe that what they are sharing is consequential
- believe that you care
- are willing to make themselves vulnerable
- trust you more

It's hard to add more to the conversation regarding why good listening is important, but there is a benefit to it that is less obvious: good listening better enables you to determine what is and isn't important contemporaneously.

There is a difference between listening to someone who is struggling, or who needs some help, or who just needs a friend versus having conversations about real or potential problems, opportunities, successes, failures, etc. This is next level listening. Listening with the goal of categorizing the information you are receiving (e.g., urgent, important but not urgent, not important, and "Let me think about it").

Quiet, confident, and humble leadership is becoming more and more of a lost art because so many are so anxious to tell others how much they know. That is not strong leadership. Unfettered listening and reflecting builds trust and is an outcome of strong leadership. Life is not a debate or a rhetoric course. Listen to understand. Listen to empathize. Listen to grow.

Another real and formidable enemy of good, active listening is time. It takes valuable time to listen actively and to contemplate, and time, unfortunately, is one of those things in short supply for school leaders. It is the one thing that we have ultimate control over, but also the thing that can easily slips through our fingers if we are not careful.

Executive leaders, like superintendents, often have people who monitor and protect their time for them, but most school leaders don't have this luxury. They have to manage their time themselves and determine how best to use this finite resource.

Suggestion: Don't allow things that are not important to take up space in your mind. Easier said than done, but absolutely necessary not only for your professional life, but also for your time at home and your own mental health. This is one of those lessons that seasoned school administrators learn over time: if it is not important, forget it and move on, or maybe delegate it to someone else.

The awful truth regarding school leaders is that their home lives often suffer as a result of the time and emotional energy they expend at school, or while thinking about school. Take inventory of what is most important to you and remember to maintain those pieces at the top of the list as sacred. They are the untouchables: your family, your faith, and maintaining your physical and mental health should all take precedence over the latest round of drama at school.

Finally, there is a saying: 99 percent of the things we worry about never happen. As human beings, we worry about things we cannot control. As school leaders we worry about things that we can't control *and* plenty of things that will never happen. We need to consistently take comfort in the fact that we have done our best, have acted professionally and appropriately, and have put the needs of our students first.

REFLECT/CONNECT

Reflect: There is great value in stopping, listening, and not speaking. You don't have all the answers, so commit yourself to listening for understanding, not for responding. It's hard, especially if you don't begin by asking yourself what you can learn through conversation and collaboration.

Connect: Share your reflections and experiences with a community of courageous leaders just like you by using social media.

Chapter 5

What to Think

If I want your opinion, I'll give it to you.

—Samuel Goldwyn

It is not our job to teach kids what to think. That is the responsibility of the parent. Our job should be to teach kids *how* to think and more specifically how to evaluate, interpret, synthesize, draw conclusions, deduce, and think critically.

One could make the case that sharing chunks of information with kids and then asking them to regurgitate what they've heard *is* teaching them how to think. It isn't, and in many cases, it's not "teaching" at all, and the result is most certainly not the ability to think but instead to hear and remember. We've got to continue to work to change this paradigm because we are not training future *Jeopardy!* contestants.

The headlines offered by various news sources should leave no question in any of our minds that each news source endeavors to make us think a certain way, to accept its version of reality without actually digging deep enough to get to the impartial truth. By now, each of us as educated adults should be able to engage in abstract, objective thought—but we ought to worry as to whether or not we are preparing our students to do the same.

Raising and teaching kids to think for themselves with a willingness to defend a position and to express themselves in multiple ways will never go out of style, no matter how much multiple choice testing we subject them to. Likewise, recognizing that individual differences are normal and healthy, respecting the views of others, even if we don't agree with them, projecting kindness and generosity, and caring for one another is the magic sauce for developing courageous future leaders. What else is there?

In the movie *The Paper Chase*, Professor Kingsfield's description of the Socratic method very nicely correlates with the subject of this chapter:

At times you may feel that you have found the correct answer. I assure you that this is a total delusion on your part; you will never find the correct absolute and final answer. In my classroom there is always another question; another question that follows your answer.

We do brain surgery here. You teach yourselves the law but I train your mind. You come in here with a skull full of mush and you leave thinking like a lawyer.

Our students are not all going to Harvard Law School, but they should all end up with the ability to think for themselves.

REFLECT/CONNECT

Reflect: An educator's job is to teach kids how to think and help them acquire the skills they will actually need. Think of an educator who embodies this mission. Give them a special shout out and some sincere positive reinforcement.

Connect: Share your reflections and experiences with a community of courageous leaders just like you by using social media.

Chapter 6

The Deafening Silence
of Our Outrage

If you want to be a real human being—a real woman, a real man—you cannot tolerate things which put you to indignation, to outrage. You must stand up. I always say to people, "Look around; look at what makes you unhappy, what makes you furious, and then engage yourself in some action."

—Stephane Hessel

After each school shooting we hear and experience what we've heard and experienced after all other school shootings: an influx of thoughts and prayers and not much else. A politician from Texas upped the ante and wrote that he and his wife are now "fervently" praying for the children and families of Uvalde, Texas. Surely the families of the twenty-one victims are comforted and relieved by such a courageous gesture.

Within two weeks of the horrific tragedy in Uvalde, thirteen additional school shootings took place in the United States and a total of forty-two mass shootings. In fact, there was a school shooting in New Orleans three days after the Uvalde incident where three people were killed. Shootings have become so common that those with smaller numbers of victims don't receive much coverage. *The Washington Post* reported that since 1999 at least 185 children, educators, and other people have been killed in assaults, and another 369 have been injured in school shootings.

Since Uvalde we've heard the typical and intellectually dishonest refrain regarding "Why?" and "What's to be done?" about school shootings. Here is a partial list of the causes:

• These are mental health issues, not gun issues.

- Laws that are on the books aren't being enforced so why should more be passed?
- Legally owning a firearm (in any quantity) is protected under the Second Amendment (key term here being "amendment," where thirty-three have been proposed by Congress).
- The national response to COVID-19 (e.g., virtual learning, vaccinations, mask-wearing) has caused an uptick in the number of school shootings.
- The doors to the schools should have been locked.
- All school building should have had armed guards.
- The shooter grew up without a father.
- The shooter didn't go to church.
- The shooter used drugs.
- The shooter made threats via social media that were ignored.

It seems that many people are willing to point to *anything* other than easy access to guns as to why so many mass shootings occur in the United States. Anything. Other countries surely have folks with mental health issues, who use drugs, who had one parent, who don't go to church, who had to wear masks. So why are the overwhelming majority of these murders occurring in the United States?

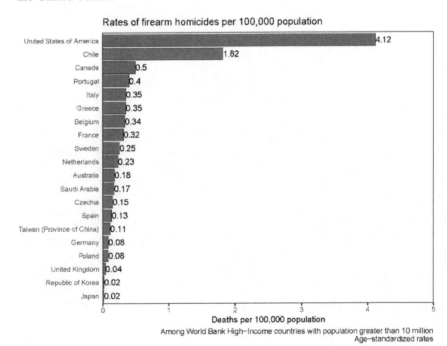

Figure 6.1. Rates of firearm homicides per 100,000 population

Based on trend data, here's what can be predicted: There will be significantly more school shootings unless meaningful action is taken. Sadly, these shootings have become inevitable, and their frequency has made many callous to the deaths of innocent children.

We need to be very clear and very honest about what is happening. Children's bodies are being torn apart by bullets often fired from high-powered automatic and semiautomatic weapons that are designed to kill people. Destroyed families, traumatized children and adults, and inescapable guilt will continue to permeate communities that simply want a safe place for their kids to go to school. We will continue to clean the floors of classrooms, cafeterias, and hallways of the pooled blood of those who we were not able to protect because we couldn't completely shield them from harm.

Individuals who should not have access to these types of weapons, including those treated for mental health issues, or who were previously convicted of crimes involving weapons and/or domestic abuse, continue to have easy access. Can we at least agree that they shouldn't? Is requiring someone to wait thirty, sixty, or ninety days to purchase a weapon so that a background check can be conducted that controversial? Is increasing the age when an individual can purchase firearms, including assault weapons, from eighteen to twenty-one be that difficult to support? Many politicians seem to think so. An eighteen-year-old can't go into a bar an order a beer, but they can purchase an automatic weapon legally and easily. Does this make sense?

Even in schools that are staffed with full-time armed officers, innocent children will continue to be murdered. We need to be honest with ourselves and acknowledge that if someone with assault weapons wants to kill children and teachers, they will find a way, either inside or outside of our buildings, to do so.

One ill-conceived idea to deter a shooter from entering a school is to design the building with only one exit and one entrance with armed guards stationed at each. This would be helpful unless, of course, there's a bomb threat, a fire alarm goes off, or someone figures out that it will take a long time for kids to file in and out of buildings with just one entrance or exit. Why not just build a moat around every school in the county and install drawbridges?

If our government and elected officials won't take the necessary and courageous steps to protect our kids and staffs, here are some eventualities that we could very easily see take root in the not-so-distant future (aside from additional shootings):

- More armed officers inside, outside, and on top of buildings
- A renewed push to arm teachers
- A stop to outside activities for fear of sniper-like shootings

- Vestibules created whereby buses can stop in front of building and kids can enter without being exposed
- No longer allowing anyone but children and staff to enter buildings

Our schools will conceivably become fortresses. Instead of dealing with the gun accessibility issue, it seems to make more sense to those opposed to gun control to build and/or redesign schools similar to the way that prisons are constructed. If you think these are far-fetched predictions, think again.

School leadership will do whatever it takes to protect kids if our government will not. It wasn't that long ago that armed officers in schools seemed unnecessary, even over-the-top. "Buzz-in" systems and identification software were met with some resistance and fear of "privacy" invasion. Propping doors open to let air in was actually considered healthy, but now it is forbidden. Hostile intruder training and drills were and are a good thing but seemed very unlikely to ever be employed.

Today, we are in a new place in terms of school security, but the national response has remained inept and mostly nonexistent.

No one should have to experience this sort of trauma. No one should have to experience what the families of these beautiful souls in Uvalde, Texas, have experienced.

On the bright side, there was a great deal of talk about a bipartisan response to the murders in Uvalde. There was optimism and a long overdue recognition that about 85 percent of the country favors background checks as a minimum response. What took so long? Why so much resistance and concern about making someone wait to purchase weapons somehow violates their constitutional rights? The twenty-one people murdered in Uvalde lost *all* of their rights in an instant. All of them. Life, liberty, and the pursuit of happiness.

One resource theoretically at our disposal is to disband face-to-face school instruction in favor of virtual learning until significant steps are taken at the state and federal levels to keep guns out of the hands of people who shouldn't have them, or perhaps a ban on assault weapons. Admittedly, this idea has zero chance of broad implementation based on the current political environment, but such drastic suggestions will get people's attention.

We have to ask some very difficult questions, the first being whether or not our schools are indeed safe places based on the number and frequency of these shootings. One could very easily argue that they are not.

Our muted response and lack of demonstrated outrage regarding these issues is beyond discouraging. The silence is deafening and somewhat surprising considering that much of the rhetoric centers on "what else" schools can do to keep kids safe.

It is becoming clearer that we are expected to take whatever steps are necessary to ensure the safety of our kids, but those in power seem to be hoping that this sort of sickening violence will be eradicated under an avalanche of fervent prayers. Most believe in the power of prayer, but we also must recognize that "faith without works is dead." Taking a courageous stand and advocating for the safety of kids should be a no-brainer, but it does not seem to be for many of the folks we elect to represent us and our families.

Reflect: What is more important than keeping kids safe in school? Anything? What is preventing you from being more outspoken regarding the need to keep kids safe in schools?

Connect: Share your reflections, experiences, and ideas with a community of courageous leaders just like you, then take action either individually or collectively.

Chapter 7

It's Okay to Ignore

If you want to make everyone happy,
Don't be a leader. Sell ice cream.

—Steve Jobs

Take the high road, there's a lot less traffic up there.

—Dr. Phil

As seasoned adults, we understand that *being an adult* is hard work. Four components of adulthood have arguably risen to the top in terms of importance: honesty, responsibility, integrity, and courage. For some within school communities, these traits mean nothing. In fact, they sometimes become fodder for additional scorn. If you are a school leader, you'll relate quite well to this message shared with a school community in Northern Virginia:

Over the past two years (the COVID-19 age), I've seen a much greater incidence of anonymous correspondence and, in some cases, correspondence coming from fictitious sources. I've received direct correspondence or correspondence through social media, whereby individuals have actually created fictitious identities in order to spread false and damaging information. Some of it is clearly political. Some of it is meant to harm the reputations of individuals within the school division—typically for no good reason. Some of it demands some sort of action on my part. Some of it is flat-out insulting—but that is not who this short message is intended for. Most of these messages are no more than sad attempts to bring attention and drama into the lives of people who are insecure, bored, desperate, and angry.

Hats off to the folks (and there are a lot of them out there) who are willing to share concerns bravely and respectfully and with their names attached. We appreciate you so very much!

It's easy to be anonymous. It's easy to weigh in on topics that you've not taken the time to understand. It's easy to lob grenades at people whom you have never met and certainly don't understand. It's easy to hit the send button from your couch. It's like someone once said: "It's amazing what people will write in their pajamas."

Unless the safety of an individual is at stake, or it is reported that a crime has been committed, ignore these communications. Don't pay any attention to them. If individuals don't have the courage or integrity to communicate with you directly, don't waste your valuable time considering or responding to this gutless form of communication.

REFLECT/CONNECT

Reflect: When you are attacked through a negative correspondence, remind yourself to take the high road and remain professional. If you allow the attacker to bring you down, they win.

Connect: Share your reflections and experiences with a community of courageous leaders just like you by using social media.

SECTION TWO

Fixing the Things That Need to Be Fixed

Step one: Face the harsh realities.
Step two: Consider the unthinkable.
Step three: Take risks because all they can do is fire you.

Chapter 8

Follow the Money, Because It Is about the Money!

Don't let anyone tell you that standardized tests are not accurate measures. The truth of the matter is they offer a remarkably precise method for gauging the size of the houses near the school where the test was administered.

—Alfie Kohn

Don't let anyone ever tell you that, when it comes to the quality of our schools, money does not matter. It does. There is an old and very wise adage that goes like this: If someone tells you that it is "not about the money," chances are it *is* about the money. This is a deliciously ironic and frighteningly accurate truth that is typically applied to professional athletes who jump from one team to another. For some reason, however, the average taxpaying, law-abiding, educated citizen is often under the impression that the influence of wealth on the quality of education is minimal. It isn't. It has a tremendous and undeniable impact.

Some people like to think that teachers do what they do because they love teaching and would probably do it for free. While this may be true for a fair amount of teachers, the vast majority are just like all the rest of us: They have families, mortgages, tuition to cover, and other bills to pay. Money matters to them, and the difference of even $5,000 in their salary is significant.

It would be hypocritical for any of us to begrudge a teacher who chooses to move to a wealthier, better-paying school district in order to make more money. Nevertheless, the consequences are that good teachers leave needy schools for better opportunities. The same logic holds true for school administrators, bus drivers, custodians, maintenance workers, and school nutrition workers. In short, money matters.

Take another look at Alfie Kohn's quote above. Does it resonate with you? Well, it should. Many data sources report that students in affluent schools consistently achieve at much greater levels than do their poorer counterparts. Money does matter. Teacher pay, the quality of facilities, PTA/PTO fundraising, instructional resources, and the availability of technology do matter. We have to stop blaming the kids, the neighborhood, single parenting, and so on and focus on what we can control. We have definitive control over just one thing: our time with the kids and how we use it. It is folly to think that we have significant control over anything else.

REFLECT/CONNECT

Reflect: We have definitive control over just one thing: our time with the kids and how we use it. What are some examples of creative and courageous use of time? Identify one way instructional schedules could be altered to allow for a more positive impact on student learning.

Connect: Share your reflections and experiences with a community of courageous leaders just like you by using social media.

Chapter 9

It's (Really) Okay to Fail

Failure should be our teacher, not our undertaker. Failure is delay, not defeat. It is a temporary detour, not a dead end. Failure is something we can avoid only by saying nothing, doing nothing, and being nothing.

—Denis Waitley

People tend to vividly remember where they were and what they were doing when tragic events occurred. Whether it was the Kennedy assassination, the *Columbia* space shuttle tragedy, or 9/11, people maintain vivid memories of those events. Steven remembered, for example, exactly where he was and what he was doing the first time he realized that he was not as "smart" as the other kids. In fact, Steven remembered thinking that he was dumb and that he was not like everyone else. Those memories still haunt him.

Steven was told during the summer between second and third grade that he would be attending a new school, not because he wanted to, his parents wanted him to, or because his family had changed residences, but because he was struggling in school, and someone at some point decided that he needed more specialized educational services.

Initially, he didn't think or care much about the change. He did have to ride the "little bus," but that didn't bother him at first. His new school seemed fine, and he made new friends quickly.

The following summer his mother hinted that he might be returning to his old school, and he was excited! He was becoming more and more sensitive to the teasing by some of his neighborhood pals. It seemed that riding the little bus to school wasn't a cool, normal thing, and some of the not-so-innocent teasing that he was experiencing was damaging. Still, Steven wasn't traumatized by the kids—just annoyed. The traumatization came at the hands of adults—one in particular.

One fall morning, Steven and his classmate Donna were called to the office. They were quietly escorted into a room where a man whom they had

41

never seen before sat at a desk. He was an older, balding "gentleman" who wore glasses and a scowl. He did not acknowledge their entrance. Steven and Donna sat down in two chairs directly in front of his desk and waited. After a few moments, the man spoke: "Donna, spell a word for me." She thought for a moment and then, with a smile on her face, said, "Cat. C-A-T. Cat." The man behind the desk was unimpressed. He said, "Can you spell a longer word?"

Donna's smile gradually faded, replaced by a look of sheer embarrassment. She sat quietly for a moment and said nothing.

After what seemed like an eternity, she spoke: "No, I can't." The man said nothing at first and instead jotted down a few notes. After a moment or two he looked at Donna with the same uninterested gaze and said, "You can return to class." Without saying a word, humiliated, Donna exited the room.

Just the balding man and Steven remained in the room. Steven felt bad for Donna, but what could he do? He knew she could spell longer words. Why didn't she? "*Anyone* can spell *cat*, for crying out loud," he thought to himself.

The man eventually looked at Steven and spoke: "Please spell a word for me."

This was his chance! His foolproof strategy was to spell the longest word that he could think of, totally impress the grumpy guy whom he did not know, and then be returned immediately to Murphy Ranch Elementary on a big, long bus. He grinned confidently and then said, "Mother. M-O-T-H-E-R. Mother."

Steven smiled broadly and was extremely proud of myself. Hey, how many eight-year-olds could spell "mother"? But, as you might have guessed, the bespectacled man was not impressed. Steven quickly surmised that perhaps all eight-year-olds could spell "mother."

"Can you spell a longer word?" the man asked.

Looking, back, Steven is certain he could have spelled a longer word. If the man had asked him to spell "December" or "Mississippi," for example, he certainly would have nailed it. He didn't and instead left the choosing to Steven. Steven thought for a moment and drew a blank. "No, I can't" was his shamed reply. The man jotted down a few notes and offered a look of disgust. "You can return to class" were the parting words from the man whom *he would never see again.*

Steven is now in his late fifties. He's earned a master's degree in curriculum and instruction and a doctorate in educational leadership. He's enjoyed a successful career as an educator, having served as a high school social studies teacher, high school principal, and a public school superintendent. He is an adjunct professor, teaching future school administrators, for a prestigious Washington, DC, area university. He's been happily married for more than thirty years and has two great boys who were good students and happy kids and are now successful professionals. However, a part of him is still ashamed and embarrassed to write or talk about his time as a special education student.

But he shouldn't be. Those experiences, gratefully, have helped shaped him into the educator he is today.

There is no cookie-cutter formula to become a leader. They come in all shapes and sizes, all backgrounds, and with various gifts and talents. They also come with weaknesses, flaws, biases, and insecurities. All of them. As you have probably experienced, sometimes individuals selected for leadership positions have no business being there, and many who could be outstanding leaders are never given the chance or simply don't have the confidence or desire to pursue those roles.

This is unfortunate because schools need great leaders, and it seems that fewer and fewer people are pursuing careers in educational leadership. Who can blame them? It is tough work with few accolades and lousy pay— especially when you calculate hourly rates—and is painfully isolating. If you think that it is lonely at the top, it is. No one who is not in teaching will ever understand what your professional life is like. We all, ultimately, have to take comfort and satisfaction knowing that we are helping the kids we teach, their parents, and our staffs.

REFLECT/CONNECT

Reflect: Is there a method of evaluation or student "tracking" in your school or school system that is ineffective, even harmful? Get rid of it. Work with staff to identify authentic, unconventional methods of measuring student needs, abilities, and successes.

Connect: Identify someone you know, a colleague for example, whom you believe would be a great leader. Tell them and encourage them to consider leadership opportunities. Moreover, share with them specifically what qualities you've observed that led you to this conclusion.

Chapter 10

From Brittle to Resilient

Most things are good, and they are the strongest things; but there are evil things too, and you are not doing a child a favor by trying to shield him from reality. The important thing is to teach a child that good can always triumph over evil.

—Walt Disney

Brittle children often become brittle adults. They are frequently raised by parents who feel as though they must intervene on behalf of their children whenever a problem, no matter how minor, occurs. They make excuse after excuse for their kids.

If they get a bad grade, it is because the teacher didn't teach the information correctly. If their child gets into a fight, it is always the other child's fault. If their child isn't named the starting shortstop on the baseball team, it is because the coach is biased. If their high school senior doesn't get into a prestigious university, it is because the school system failed him. If the child has excessive absences, it is because the school is creating "stress" in the life of the child and, as a result, becomes ill at the thought of going to school.

Our instincts tell us to help the students in these situations, but the parents are typically the problem, and they are often much more difficult to help.

If you've been a public school administrator for any significant length of time, then you've participated in conferences with parents who MUST solve the problems of their children without ever requiring their children to take responsibility and ownership for their own actions. They swoop in to fix the problem and then swoop out, temporarily confident that they have truly advocated for their child. The end results are often children, young adults, and grown men and women who are unable to cope with life's challenges and, rather than benefiting from the removal of obstacles by parents, actually face the additional hurdle of never truly developing resiliency.

45

Brittle children leave home for college and often return a short time later. Nationally, roughly 50 percent of students who enroll in college as recent high school graduates never finish (Hansen, 2021).

Students who leave high school in a brittle state, already burned out by being overparented, and having never developed genuine resiliency, will struggle mightily in the postsecondary school universe. College dropout statistics support this. By shifting our focus toward fostering resiliency and by providing parents with honest and sometimes brutal support, their children will develop into confident, self-advocating students and adults.

We've got a parenting crisis on our hands that has nothing to do with neglect, substance abuse, physical abuse, or indifference. The problem is just the opposite. We are raising children who lack resilience and who, when challenged, seize up and give up.

It should not come as a shock to anyone how many students do not finish college. It is an endemic result of the strategy that many parents have adopted for how best to raise children, and it is crippling many futures.

You may have read the story about the parents who allowed their children to walk alone to and from a park about a mile or so from their home. A concerned neighbor was alarmed at seeing small children walking

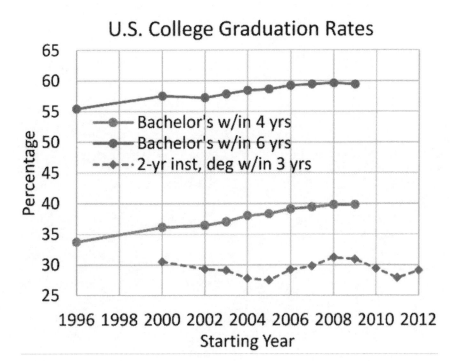

Figure 10.1. National Center of Education Statistics

unaccompanied and called the police who, in turn, paid a visit to the parents. When the parents explained that they routinely allowed their children to walk to and from the park, Social Services was contacted, and they threatened to take the children from the home. The parents, to their credit, argued that they were teaching their children independence and self-sufficiency, precisely as *they* had been taught.

What has caused parents to become so protective? Child abductions are actually down 40 percent since 1997 (FBI, 2020). So why has "stranger danger" become a parenting mantra? Many of us were raised in neighborhoods where, particularly during the summer months, we left the house in the morning to play, came home for lunch, went back out to play, and came home when we were called for dinner, usually at dusk. This laissez-faire approach to supervision is unheard of now and might just earn you a visit from a community agency.

It is unlikely that anyone who has a significant background as an educator doesn't know what "helicopter parenting" is, but for those who may not, here is a great definition by Kathleen Vinson:

> Helicopter parenting is a term used to describe the phenomenon of a growing number of parents—obsessed with their children's success and safety—who vigilantly hover over them, sheltering them from mistakes, disappointment, or risks; insulating them from the world around them. Some helicopter parents may even cross the line into unethical areas, such as unknowingly teaching their children it is acceptable to plagiarize, falsify records, or bully others to get what they want.

Sound familiar? Ever had this sort of suffocating, frustrating, and, frankly, sad experience with a parent? Recent research surrounding this topic finds that helicopter parenting now impacts *higher* education more than ever (Vinson, 2013). On reflection, it makes perfect sense. Many students are leaving our high schools completely unprepared to deal with failure, frustration, uncertainty, and, of course, independence.

If you've been in education long enough, particularly at the secondary level, you've perhaps had the experience of walking into the local fast-food restaurant and discovering that the person taking your order is one of your recent or not-so-recent graduates. It being late fall/early winter, you query the student as to why they are no longer in college. A typical, sheepish, embarrassed response is, of course, that things didn't work out and the college they had been attending really didn't care about them, or they didn't get along with their roommate, or they didn't "fit in," or they simply flunked out.

What is fascinating is that these were kids on top of the world, ready to conquer, full of confidence, and anxious to leave home. Seeing them return

"Perhaps this would feel less painful if you try focusing on your own life rather than living vicariously through mine."

Figure 10.2. Perhaps this would feel less painful

defeated, dispirited, and aimless is absolutely heartbreaking. Meno (2016) stated it this way:

> When children aren't given the space to struggle through things on their own, they don't learn to problem-solve very well. They don't learn to be confident in their own abilities, and it can affect their self-esteem. The other problem with never having to struggle is that you never experience failure and can develop an overwhelming fear of failure and of disappointing others. Both the low self-confidence and the fear of failure can lead to depression or anxiety.

The challenges parents face in the twenty-first century world are daunting, but they do the best that they can. Parents send us the best they have. No matter how difficult or frustrating a situation can become, we are dealing with someone's precious offspring. As administrators, we can't ever lose sight of this. We are talking about someone's kids *and* their ability as parents; however, we have a duty to help the parents, particularly the ones who are actually hurting their kid's futures by being overinvolved.

But trying to tell a parent how to raise their child is the ultimate lose-lose proposition. So how do you help?

- Be honest but kind with parents. They may not like what you have to say, but if you have built a relationship with them, they may at least listen.
- Don't back down or lower expectations, and don't let your teachers do so either. It's tougher to do than it sounds. Parents sometimes make demands and get way too involved and, as a result, they alienate just about everyone. It's okay. The goal is to help the student ultimately, not the parent. Sadly, some parents may be too far gone, so focus on the student.
- Look at the data, because it's self-explanatory. You can see in the graph shared earlier in this chapter that the number of students who never finish college is alarming. We lack evidence to make the connection between helicopter parenting and college dropouts, but common sense would suggest the connection is likely. Moreover, the pervasive attitude among parents that their children *must* attend college isn't helping.

There are so many great and well-paying careers to pursue that don't require a four-year or even two-year degree. Had to pay an electrician or HVAC repairman lately? Those services are incredibly expensive in part because so few people are choosing these paths. The stigma associated with not choosing college right out of high school is a genuine barrier, often one created by parents who want what is best for their kids but aren't aware of what else is available for their recent high school graduates.

REFLECT/CONNECT

Reflect: Reach out to a parent whom you think of as a "helicopter parent." Keeping the conversation focused on what is best for the child, suggest one way the parent could take a step back and enable their child to build resiliency.

Connect: Share your reflections and experiences with a community of courageous leaders just like you by using social media.

Chapter 11

The Assessment-Instruction Relationship

The definition of insanity is doing the same thing over and over again and getting the same result, but expecting a different one.

—Albert Einstein

For most of us the problem isn't that we aim too high and fail. It's just the opposite: We aim too low and succeed.

—Sir Ken Robinson

Figure 11.1. Climb this tree

Multiple choice, "high-stakes" standardized testing hurts students, especially those who are at risk, and it needs to be replaced. There is plenty of data available that shows we are worse off educationally as a result of a standardized testing culture, which has culminated in an instructional landscape that is "a mile wide and two inches deep." The current standardized assessment system that was designed to level the playing field for all has instead morphed into a system that, at best, prepares kids to become capable *Jeopardy!* contestants.

This is not what students deserve from us, especially "at risk" students who desperately need something different in order to escape from the inequity that our current one-size-fits-all approach promotes. We can most likely agree that there is a problem, but what to do about it is the real fodder for conversation. It is time to drop a metaphorical grenade and start over, bravely, courageously, and with a commitment to making the right choices for our kids.

How did standardized testing evolve in the United States? How has standardized testing helped to defeat the kid it was designed to help? What has been the impact of multiple-choice, standardized testing? What are the alternatives? There is intense and significant disagreement regarding the value of high-stakes standardized testing, but we've got to have an honest conversation and start making courageous choices. We can't wait any longer.

Before we go any further, we must answer the "why" question": Why is this an issue that must be addressed?

K–12 Assessment and Instruction Don't Match the Twenty-First-Century World

When asked what Google looked for in future employees, one of their executives answered this way:

> We aren't looking for people who know a lot of facts. We're Google. We have all of the facts. We are looking for people who can take an ill-defined problem and work collaboratively in order to solve it.

At least for the good folks at Google, seasoned and even successful standardized test takers are not in demand. The ability to memorize and regurgitate chunks of information is not a necessary skill set. After all, just about every adult in this country owns a computer that is typically a million times more powerful than the computers used to put a human on the moon (Puiu, 2015).

Employers are looking, instead, for problem solvers, skilled communicators, multitaskers, independent workers, team players, and abstract thinkers who can work with others in order to achieve sometimes ill-defined objectives (Isherwood, 2018). Our responsibility ought to include preparing students with the skills they need in order to better meet the demands of the tweny-first century career market and, to no lesser degree, skill set expectations associated with the military, higher education, and the trades.

We need to be striving to equip kids with a toolbox that matches the demands of our planet and then figure out the best way(s) to assess attainment.

WHAT'S WRONG WITH STANDARDIZED, MULTIPLE-CHOICE TESTING?

Here is a very typical multiple-choice question: What is the capital of the United States? A) Philadelphia B) New York C) Chicago D) None of the Above. This is an extremely primitive example, but it illustrates why a teacher might teach to a test: "Students: The capital of the United States is Washington, DC. You'll need to know that for the upcoming (fill in the blank with the appropriate state-designed assessment) test." When teachers feel immense pressure to cover all the material prior to the state assessment, they are prone to teach in chunks, which involves the sharing of factual information in smaller sections because they neatly align with content likely to be seen again on a standardized test. As a result, you end up with classroom environments where the teacher is doing almost all of the talking.

Teacher talk dominates American classrooms: the teacher is typically the one asking the questions and conveying information to the students. This is a very inefficient way to instruct kids, because they are likely not to retain what they are being taught. As a result, kids are often bored and feel no real connection to the material. In other words, they don't have ownership over their own learning. They don't see the value in it. They don't know how to apply the information or why it should be applied. They don't know how to synthesize the information or why it should be synthesized.

Researchers Robert Marzano, Debra Pickering, and Jane Pollock found that direct, lecture-oriented instruction is most impactful in regard to the retention of information, but lecturing is also vastly overused to the point that other, more diverse methods of instruction are often nonexistent in classrooms (Marzano, Pickering, and Pollock, 2001).

Students need to be asking the questions, discovering information, working together, and drawing conclusions. Today, they are often passive receptors of information being provided by the teacher. In a twenty-first-century world, teachers should be facilitators.

We have a deeply flawed K–12 assessment culture that is not serving the purpose for which it was initially created. It has evolved into an inequitable means of measuring student learning, growth, and mastery. The very students, for example, that the No Child Left Behind (NCLB) Act was designed to protect through high-stakes testing have instead been marginalized. Finite resources designated to support a failed assessment system could be much better used elsewhere. Tim Slekar, dean of the School of Education at Edgewood College, says this about the effect of testing on equity:

> We're concerned about equity in education. You will never achieve equity by spending the few resources that you have, money, on tests. Tests don't produce equity. They just show you that you have inequities. (Slekar, 2019)

It is essential to note that our current educational system is based on an instructional and institutional model that is more than 125 years old. Our first public schools were designed around an extremely limited, but at the time quite effective, method of teaching kids so that they could seamlessly matriculate into jobs that began to emerge during the Industrial Revolution. Ted Dintersmith describes the dilemma quite well:

> The 1893 model of educating students through school was successful for its time. School was designed to teach students the same subjects in the same way and train them to perform routine tasks efficiently and without error. This system helped to produce a uniform workforce for work on assembly lines. Although this model of educating students is from 1893, it has changed very little despite society changing a great deal. We know now that this system of education is obsolete; current and future jobs/careers require a more diverse skill set. Even students with strong grades and test scores are not necessarily acquiring the skills currently needed in workplaces and in society. (Dintersmith, 2018)

Where else does an innovation and design lag such as this exist? Nowhere, most likely. The corresponding assessment and accountability systems that are, of course, based on performance on high-stakes standardized tests perpetuate this problem.

It is logical to assume that, until we begin to assess differently, there will be no compelling reason to instruct differently, organize and design schools differently, or hold different expectations for students and teachers. We teach the way we assess, and the result has been chunked instruction focused on memorizing facts in bits and then remembering them just long enough to answer correctly on an inauthentic assessment.

GAPS STILL EXIST

Nationwide, there has been no significant reduction in learning achievement gaps since NCLB (Strauss, 2015), but many politicians who, by the way, are often the last people who should be dictating educational philosophy and strategy to schools, are at best reluctant to transition to a more equitable way of measuring learning, measuring growth, and judging the relative success or failure of schools.

It's worth asking why individuals who typically have no other educational and instructional background than attending schools themselves are empowered to make such important decisions regarding the education of our youth. Should they be the ones dictating educational philosophy and strategy at any level? Legislators don't question the expertise of other professionals, such as doctors. Why do they get to decide educational policy?

These comments are in no way a negative reflection on their motives, which are certainly genuine and truly reflect child centeredness. These are good people with good hearts, but we've seen the outcomes of NCLB and found that it didn't help the students and schools it was designed to support (Darling-Hammond, 2007).

In Virginia, students in third through twelfth grade are required to take at least thirty-two standardized tests, down from thirty-seven in 2019. In Finland, the global model for how public schools should be run, students take exactly one test (divided into four parts) over the entirety of their schooling (Dickinson, 2019).

Kids hate standardized tests. Teachers often leave the profession specifically because of them. Parents don't seem to understand why we give them. Interestingly, Sir Ken Robinson, international speaker on education, notes that the near epidemic rise of ADHD in the United States closely correlates with the rise of standardized testing (Robinson, 2010). Standardization of instruction, assessment, school frameworks, and time-boundedness has moved us in the wrong direction. We should be moving away from a standardized approach to schooling in general, beginning with dismantling a twentieth-century method of measuring learning.

If you were responsible for preparing someone to fly an airplane for the first time, it is unlikely that you'd administer a series of multiple-choice tests and then, assuming your student passed all of them, hand them the keys to a brand-new Cessna. A standardized approach that included little to no opportunity for practice, collaboration, observation, problem-solving, authentic engagement, and demonstrated mastery would not be appropriate, and yet we follow a standardized model of inauthentic assessment in our schools every day.

High-stakes, standardized, multiple-choice testing defeats attempts at providing equity in several ways:

1. Students aren't necessarily demonstrating what they know through multiple-choice testing. They can guess and get the answer right. In some cases, if they get the answer right, it is because they remembered

a keyword or phrase, not because they mastered the content associated with the question.

2. The tests encourage teachers to teach in chunks so that all of the material is covered prior to testing. Students are much less likely to retain information "taught" in this way. Remember: talking is not necessarily teaching.

3. Some students are simply poor test takers and would be better able to show what they have learned through a more authentic assessment, like a research paper, a project, or a portfolio. I'll be sharing more about alternate assessment methods later in the chapter.

4. There are a myriad of test prep websites and other resources available to parents who have the time, money, and motivation necessary to take advantage of them. More power to them if this is what they decide is best for their children, but, of course, many students do not have this kind of support at home. For their families, the money is better spent elsewhere.

5. Tests discourage innovative and interesting instructional approaches by teachers because teachers feel immense pressure to cover material, and coverage is the enemy of understanding.

6. Tests encourage comparisons and additional inequities based on race, socioeconomic status, and disability. As Liberty High School's (Virginia) assistant principal and head basketball coach Lauren Milburn observes, "It's disgusting that we base minimum testing pass rates on things such as race. . . . The system is essentially saying that if you're Asian you should pass these tests but if you're Black you should not. The inequity and absolute insanity of those minimum pass rates is disturbing."

7. Test prep software and intervention programming designed to help students pass multiple-choice standardized tests is a multibillion-dollar industry (Broflowski, 2020). These sorts of programs are often purchased with federal Title I funds. Imagine if these funds could be redirected toward manipulatives, field trips, materials used for project-based learning, guest lecturers, and so on.

A BRIEF HISTORY OF STANDARDIZED TESTS

In 1926, the first SATs were administered to students across the United States as written exams. They were designed to measure precisely what students knew and, of equal importance, to assess whether they could clearly and convincingly demonstrate what they had mastered. This is a form of authentic assessment.

Figure 11.2. The IBM 805 circa 1937

There is great value in determining exactly what kids know and whether they can synthesize information, clearly and concisely express thoughts, and then apply what they have learned. Multiple-choice tests for the most part cannot accomplish this. Although contemporary SAT and state standardized tests include a written component, the majority of state standardized testing is of the multiple-choice variety.

It's worth taking a look at how we got into this mess to begin with before examining ways to get out of it. The following time line helps to demonstrate why and how high-stakes standardized testing exploded in the United States and why the need for faster, cheaper, and more easily comparable data became necessary:

- From 1901 through 1925, the College Board administered essay tests covering nine subjects. The expectation was, of course, that students would demonstrate what they had learned, authentically and in a written format. However, very few students participated in these assessments (Jacobsen, 2006).
- The first Scantron machine was introduced in 1937. It was designed to score tests quickly and inexpensively. Reading, punctuation correction, grammatical correction, and the addition of teacher comments is very time-consuming. It is undeniable that the ease associated with scoring multiple-choice tests has added to the popularity of these machines.
- In 1957, the successful launch by the Soviets of the Sputnik satellite got our attention. There followed a renewed and intense focus on science education and upper-level math (Dean, 2007).
- The war in Vietnam heightened the importance of test scores following a significant college enrollment increase between 1966 and 1972 as many students sought to avoid conscription.
- A connection between proficiency in math and science and the future of our nation's economy was highlighted. "America was at extreme economic risk largely because of 'bad schools'" (Meir, 2000).

Top 10 Most In-Demand Soft Skills

(Based on % of members with skill who were hired into a new job)

1	Communication	57.9%
2	Organization	56.5%
3	Teamwork	56.4%
4	Always Punctual	55.9%
5	Critical Thinking	55.8%
6	Social Skills	55.8%
7	Creativity	55.0%
8	Interpersonal Communication	55.0%
9	Adaptability	54.9%
10	Friendly Personality	54.6%

Figure 11.3. Top Ten Most In-Demand

- Between 1960 and 1970, the number of high school graduates in the United States increased by one million, and the number of high school juniors and seniors taking the SAT tripled during the same period (Turnbull, 1985).
- Between 1963 and 1977, SAT scores steadily declined in the United States (Turnbull, 1985).
- Grade inflation in colleges and universities became a significant issue in the 1960s and 1970s as educational leaders began to suspect that professors were inflating grades in order to allow students to avoid the draft (Yardley, 1997).
- The 1983 A Nation at Risk study found that the United States lagged far behind most modernized nations in terms of math, science, and reading.
- The No Child Left Behind Act put testing and accountability on steroids. On the upside it focused on the achievement of all students. The downside was that schools, teachers, and students were judged almost exclusively on the outcomes of standardized test scores (primarily multiple choice).

Granted, we must walk a fine line. Test scores are important, and standardized testing results are the law of the land in terms of school accreditation, graduation eligibility, and how we are judged not only by our communities but also by our state and local governments. But our charge is to prepare students for the future, not the past. Our current instructional and assessment framework was designed according to the goals of saving time and money, creating easily comparable data sets, and applying a system of instructional and assessment equality that essentially ignored the importance of providing equity. Equity and equality are not the same thing. Standardized models based on equality haven't worked in schools.

People like me are partly to blame because we helped create a generation of educators who were inducted to believe that attaining good test scores was the ultimate prize instead of authentic student learning and assessment. And once upon a time, that may have worked, but times have changed. And now is the time for education to evolve.

We are now tasked with changing a culture that has evolved over multiple generations. Politicians, school leaders, teachers, and parents must now be convinced that test scores are just one way to measure student learning. Building trust that we will support attempts to innovate and assess creatively will take courage and dedication. We must make courageous choices as we move forward in support of more reliable, authentic, and realistic ways of measuring student growth and learning.

We know what to do, but these questions remain:

- Do we have the courage needed to allow students to take ownership of their own learning?
- Will administrators allow teachers to innovate without focusing so heavily on the coverage of information and standardized test results?
- Will school boards hire superintendents who have the courage to endorse authentic student engagement and assessment as the preferred culture rather than multiple-choice testing outcomes?
- Will teachers stretch, innovate, plan, collaborate, and abandon ineffective methods of instruction and assessment?

It is important that you know exactly where you stand in regard to standardized testing. Does the current system related to high-stakes testing help or hurt kids and teachers? What do you think? What do you believe? When you interview for a principalship, for example, assessment questions are likely to be asked. How will you answer?

One really good answer: "If you are looking for a school leader who will be focused solely on raising test scores, you should not hire me. That will not and cannot be my primary focus. I will be focused on the provision of engaging instruction and authentic learning for kids, and good test scores will follow. Content can be taught in many different ways including, but most definitely not limited to, lecture and direct instruction." There are plenty of ways to raise test scores that are not necessarily good for kids, especially when overused (i.e., practice tests, intervention software, and teaching to the tests and/or state blueprints).

ASSESSMENT AND INSTRUCTION: WHAT TRUMPS WHAT?

At this point in the chapter, you may be asking yourself what, exactly, assessment has to do with instruction. In other words, why so much about the need to alter the way we instruct kids when the overarching theme of the chapter centers on revamping the way we assess learning? The simple answer is that teachers teach the way they assess, and the current method used to assess students is flawed.

The most important element to bringing about real and meaningful change is thus recruiting, hiring, training, generously compensating, and retaining outstanding teachers. The quality of teachers and teaching is always going to be the most important element of our ability to instruct authentically, engage students, and equip them with the skills they need to be successful in practically any setting. We know this, but we intentionally handcuff teachers by placing unreasonable demands on their time, often because we have no choice (e.g., state-mandated assessments), but sometimes we do have a choice.

The pressures associated with asking teachers and administrators to do things that do not promote learning keep growing. Teachers know it. They recognize it when they are asked to sacrifice authentic instruction for rote compliance, and they resent it—and none of us should blame them.

REFLECT/CONNECT

Reflect: What are some ways you can unshackle teachers and enable them to innovate without focusing so heavily on the coverage of information and standardized test results? How can you free them?

Connect: Share your reflections and experiences with a community of courageous leaders just like you by using social media.

Chapter 12

We Started This Mess and Now We Have to Clean It Up!

The greatest enemy to understanding is coverage.

—Howard Gardner

According to the Gates Foundation report The Silent Epidemic (Bridgeland, DiIulio, and Morison, 2006), the reasons most often cited by school dropouts for their decision to quit school are boredom and a lack of challenging coursework. Much further down the list is instructional rigor. In other words, school isn't too difficult for kids; it's just too boring, and we are to blame.

Many instructors and school leaders are trapped in coverage mode: they must get through the formal curriculum because of high-stakes, high-accountability, and state-standardized assessment programs. We teach it, and then the kids forget most of it over the summer. This is a cycle we need to continue to dismantle.

Teaching primarily facts, teaching quickly, ensuring the coverage of material, and providing multiple-choice benchmark tests that mirror state standardized tests have become essential teaching strategies; whether students are actually learning is a question that remains to be answered.

Howard Gardner's (1993) highly influential study regarding multiple intelligences describes and supports the value of multiple teaching strategies by discussing how individual learners learn best. A precursor to this study was Benjamin Bloom's and colleague's (1956) *Taxonomy of Educational Objectives*, most commonly known as Bloom's Taxonomy, a groundbreaking work that identified six levels associated with the learning process, from the lowest to the highest cognition levels. Bloom et al. found that most classroom instruction occurs at the lowest cognition levels, namely knowledge and comprehension. Without variety, students and educators are doomed.

The immense pressure to "cover material" rather than provide authentic learning opportunities for students eager to pursue active learning has sucked the marrow out of potentially engaging classrooms.

Cunningham and Nogle (1996) found that instructional variety significantly increased student achievement levels. These findings were supported by Marzano's more comprehensive study of multiple instructional strategies (Marzano, 1998; Marzano, Gaddy, and Dean, 2000; Marzano, Pickering, and Pollock, 2001).

The use of multiple strategies is critical to the enhancement of student learning and promotes authentic engagement, but we already know this. However, if teachers do not believe that they have the ability to bring about learning in all students, or that all students can achieve at high levels, then an argument can be made that the variety of instruction that a teacher brings to the classroom will be severely restricted by the teacher's self-perceptions and their perceptions of students. So here is where we must examine the concept of teacher efficacy.

Personal teacher efficacy (PTE) is the belief, by teachers, that they have the ability to bring about success in students. Efficacious teachers believe that students, no matter their backgrounds, can learn and be successful. Moreover, they believe that the relationship between students and teachers is a joint venture necessary for ultimate success. The uniqueness of efficacious teachers is that they believe not only that all students can be successful, but also that they as teachers have what it takes to generate student success.

General teacher efficacy (GTE) deals with teachers' perceptions about their ability to teach children while taking into consideration student characteristics that teachers have little or no control over. PTE, on the other hand, deals with teachers' beliefs that, if they try hard enough, they can reach any student *regardless of factors that teachers have no control over.*

Teachers who believe that external factors that children bring to school (home environment, socioeconomic conditions, etc.) have negative effects on student achievement are said to have lower GTE efficacy. In other words, they believe some children will not be impacted by teaching no matter how good it is.

So, let's combine all these pieces into a leadership plan for courageous school administrators:

- Allow, expect, and provide training so teachers can teach in a variety of ways. Build trust by not focusing on standardized test results. Instead, create an environment in your school that focuses on authentic learning, variety of instruction, authentic assessment of learning, and teaching skills that promote problem-solving, teamwork, effective communication, and deep-thinking.

- Build efficacy among staff. Encourage them. Train them. Build in opportunities for teachers to observe master teachers. Be their cheerleader. Recognize success and allow them to learn from failures and not be punished because of them.
- Hire the people you feel can connect with kids and are willing to take risks and, unfortunately, jettison those who simply cannot or will not make these adjustments. This is one of those harsh realities we as leaders all have to face: the need to help those who maybe should have never become teachers in the first place. Educators are very good to one another and for good reason. It's one of those occupations that only those who have done it, and done it right, can understand.

Nationally, instances of teacher "dismissal for cause" stand at about 2.1 percent. With a national teacher shortage upon us, that number is likely to decrease.

It is important to understand that our first response to any struggling teacher should be direct and consistent support. The arbitrary dismissal of teachers is never appropriate. We are in the midst of a teacher shortage, so we have to provide as much support as possible for teachers *and* recognize when teachers ultimately are doing more harm than good. No one wants to be a bad teacher and it is the responsibility of the school leader to help, support, and *encourage*. However, we also have a responsibility to help some discover new and more rewarding opportunities elsewhere.

REFLECT/CONNECT

Reflect: Most everyone agrees that we need to make choices that are in the best interest of kids, but sometimes those choices include some degree of risk. How much of a risk are you willing to take? Are you willing to write an op-ed about the virtues and importance of equity in your schools? Or perhaps lobby to limit the number and influence of standardized tests?

Connect: Share your reflections and experiences with a community of courageous leaders just like you by using social media.

Chapter 13

It's Here and It's Real

Educators are the only people who lose sleep over other people's kids.

—Nicholas A. Ferroni

The impending teacher shortage is the most critical education issue we will face in the next decade.

—David Price

The national teacher shortage has arrived. To make matters much worse, the number of college students choosing teaching as a career continues to dwindle while the demand for teachers continues to grow. Old educators like me were warned many years ago about an impending shortage, the lens being inevitable baby boomer retirements. We, like most school divisions, attend dozens of teacher job fairs each year, but we have found attendance waning.

The shortage is real and, unless we act decisively and creatively, it will only get worse. The people who will suffer as a result of this shortage are, of course, our students. The long-term impact could be catastrophic for our communities in general, and the most obvious solution doesn't seem so obvious anymore. Increasing teacher pay is certainly an enticement, but we are seeing even the highest-paying school divisions in our state dealing with the same shortages. So paying teachers more is important but doesn't seem to be the silver bullet we seek.

Recently, a group of superintendents from Virginia were tasked with creating potential solutions. Here are some of the proposed strategies—they may sound familiar:

* College loan forgiveness
* Tax breaks

Projected Teacher Supply and Demand

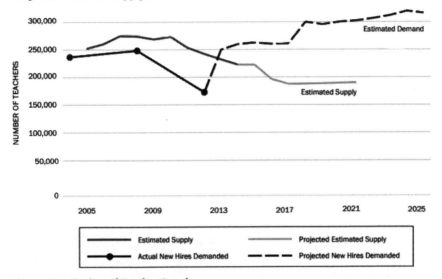

Figure 13.1. Projected Teacher Supply

- Housing assistance
- Signing and loyalty bonuses
- Limiting what we expect from teachers to teaching
- Providing more decision-making authority in schools

Most of these strategies are expensive, potentially very expensive, but the instructional alternatives associated with not having enough teachers are sparse. Widespread virtual instructional models still have a long way to go until they and. friendly models still present obstacles that must be addressed, not the least of which is the fact that virtual learning is never going to replace the fidelity and effectiveness of in-person, face-to-face instruction for most students. However, there is another solution that gets very little attention but is monumentally important.

There are many different opinions regarding why the national teacher shortage exists and is most certainly does exist. As we examine the national landscape regarding teachers and teaching in general, it makes sense to ask a somewhat rhetorical question: Who would want to be a teacher right now? Have you seen how teachers are being treated?

Teachers are an indispensable national resource but are not treated as such. Teachers need not only more money from us but also our praise. We need to elevate them to a level commensurate with the value they add to our communities. Perhaps the vast majority of folks reading this agree. They do respect, appreciate, and recognize the value teachers provide and understand that their influence has no limit. It can last for generations.

Sadly, teachers sometimes have to endure revolting public comments at school board meetings, floggings via social media, and even being called "losers" by national leaders. This treatment is absolutely disgusting and unacceptable.

Teaching is hard and typically thankless work. Unless you have done it yourself, you may not be able to relate entirely. This is not an attempt, by the way, to pit teachers against any other profession. Those comparisons shouldn't be made unless you've actually walked in all those other shoes. And yet, some people will do just that even if they've not spent a single day teaching in a classroom. Why do so many feel empowered to judge teachers? It is impossible to understand.

Let's change the conversation and consider all strategies that might attract more good people to this amazing profession. Everyone wants to feel valued and appreciated, and, as the quote at the beginning of this chapter alludes to, we are entrusting these fantastic people with our own children. Let that sink in for a bit.

It is not too late to fix this problem. We can do this!

Reflect/Connect

Reflect: Other than monetary compensation, what are some ways that we can show teachers how much they are valued? How can we make the teaching profession more attractive rather than less attractive?

Connect: Share your reflections and experiences with a community of courageous leaders just like you by using social media.

Figure 13.2. Said no teacher ever

Chapter 14

It Takes Every Single One of Us

The important thing, I think, going into any organization, is that all of the principles, all of the decision-makers are pointed in the same direction, with the same motives, the same desires, and then you have a chance.

—Mike Holmgren

Doesn't it seem like we have people in our communities who hope for bad things to happen so that they can pile on? These are the people who revel in the bad news and are silent and even cynical when the news is good. We all have these folks in our communities, but we have a lot more who want us to succeed and are willing to help us thrive.

In school divisions that are able to make the transition from good to great, the whole community gets involved. Every stakeholder—parents, students, teachers, staff, community members, business leaders—gets involved. The cliché "It takes a village to raise a child" is accurate. Everyone has something to offer, something to contribute to your school division. Asking and encouraging people to look within themselves, to identify what they can contribute to your schools, is only effective if we are doing it too.

We all do things in our school divisions really well, and we provide a good product, or service, to our students and parents, but as soon as we decide we've arrived, that's when we start to calcify. If you are standing still, you are really moving backward. We've always got to be looking toward where we can improve, where we can get better. When fellow administrators, teachers, or parents come to you with a concern, the best response should be, "Do you have a recommendation or a solution?" Sometimes they do and sometimes they don't. What is always true, however, is that opening that dialogue sends this distinct and important message: *I* don't have all the answers, but maybe *we* do.

We all understand our jobs, our responsibilities, and what is required and expected of us. We don't shy away from our responsibilities, but we are

71

individuals, and we are imperfect. Cherish and respect the serious opinions and suggestions of others. We don't have to enact or agree with them as they are likely coming from several directions and from several points of view, but we ought to carefully consider what we hear.

No system, no business, and no school division will ever operate without glitches, failures, and weaknesses, which is okay as long as we are not satisfied with where we are and are willing to do something about it.

As a community, we can and should work together in positive ways to make our school division better. Unfortunately, it often feels like many in our communities are actually working against our schools because they don't like something that is being taught, don't like the superintendent, don't like the school board, don't like a principal, don't like a book that's in the library, don't like the football coach, don't want their taxes raised, don't believe in public education, etc. We are all 100 percent committed and dedicated to our schools and school divisions, and it is important to demonstrate that to our stakeholders as often as we can. We should be the main cheerleaders, encouraging all to move in the same direction. Everyone has an oar to pull, and our assumption and expectation is that we're all pulling together toward the same place.

REFLECT/CONNECT

Reflect: How can you make your mission easily recognizable and help every staff member understand how they contribute to that mission? In other words, how can you reword your mission statement in such a way that it becomes meaningful and applicable to individuals?

Connect: Share your reflections and experiences with a community of courageous leaders just like you by using social media.

SECTION THREE

Relationships, Spirituality, and "The Boss"

Why building genuine relationships, being real, and listening to Bruce Springsteen will make you a better leader.

Chapter 15

Kids Need *You!*

If we have no peace, it is because we have forgotten
that we belong to each other.

—Mother Teresa

I have three things I'd like to say today. First, while you were sleeping last night, 30,000 kids died of starvation or diseases related to malnutrition. Second, most of you don't give a shit. What's worse is that you're more upset with the fact that I said *shit* than the fact that 30,000 kids died last night.

—Tony Campolo

When Juan began teaching, fresh out of Christian high school and college, he concluded that the only option for him was employment at a Christian school, which is where he went. Juan spent five years teaching there, and it was a great experience, but it wasn't until he left Christian school that he realized how diverse the world of education truly is and how badly kids of all walks need good teachers and leaders. More specifically, educators who will build relationships with them, care about them, be consistent with them, and dare to discipline them.

He left Christian schooling not because he felt some calling to help needy kids, but because he was broke and was having a difficult time supporting his family. Juan immediately realized how much some of his public school kids needed supportive and caring people in their lives. It felt like leaving one mission field for another, but now he was earning a livable salary. He has many friends and acquaintances who chose or are choosing private schools for their kids and applauds theme for making what they felt was the best choice. More power to them! What is offensive to many educators just like Juan is the belief among some that a private school somehow provides a better education simply because it is private.

The fact is, there are bad private schools just as there are bad public schools, and there are great public schools just as there are great private schools. Attempting to compare the two is really an "apples to watermelons" scenario. The heart of the difference is more accurately described this way:

Send us your winners and we'll make winners out of them!

Or as famed college and NFL football coach Barry Switzer once said,

Some people are born on third base and go through life thinking they hit a triple.

All of us should have tremendous respect for private school teachers, especially those who teach in religious schools. They are most certainly being underpaid and overworked, but their motives are the same as any teacher in any school: helping students. But those educators who somehow believe that there is no calling for them in public schools simply because they are public are giving up on scores of kids who might benefit directly from a morally and ethically grounded teacher. Kids recognize it. It doesn't mean that they need or want proselytization; it just means that they see something revealed in you that tells them that you are different. You care about them beyond their physical and educational needs. And, the great news is, you don't have to be "religious" to do it! Just love these kids. Allow them to see it in you. It can change their lives, and it will change your life.

The longer anyone spends time with public school kids, been a public school leader, witnessed the trauma many of our students endure, seen the poverty and abuse that some experience, and, at the same time, witnessed how willing these students are to accept people of varying colors, gender identifications, sexual orientations, religious beliefs, and disabilities, the more we should be reminded that modeling behavior and attitude are just as important as actual instruction.

We are responsible for one other. We are to care for one another. Whether you are religious or not, the words of Christ regarding the need to care for each other remain powerful:

For I was hungry and you gave me something to eat, I was thirsty and you gave me something to drink, I was a stranger and you invited me in, I needed clothes and you clothed me, I was sick and you looked after me, I was in prison and you came to visit me.

Then the righteous will answer him, "Lord, when did we see you hungry and feed you, or thirsty and give you something to drink? When did we see you a stranger and invite you in, or needing clothes and clothe you? When did we see you sick or in prison and go to visit you?'" The King will reply, "Truly I tell you, whatever you did for one of the least of these brothers and sisters of mine, you did for me."

—Matthew 25: 35–40, Bible *New International Version*

How we treat these kids, how we treat each other, how we conduct ourselves matters. Take another look at the quotes at the start of this chapter. What is it that hangs you up? What are you wasting your energy on? Remember what we are here for and what is most important: student success.

We are responsible for each other. We are called to take care of each other. We are required to give to the poor and to clothe ourselves with their sufferings and needs and then do something about them. It is like Bruce Lee said: "If everyone helped his neighbor, no one would need any help."

Lastly, a comment regarding something we hear quite often: "I don't know how you deal with those kids." In the administrative world, the kids are much less of a frustration than the adults are. I suspect you are nodding your head in agreement. The kids are fine. They need to know what the boundaries are and see them consistently enforced but with kindness and patience. Kindness and patience are so much more impactful than consequences and rigidity. The kids want us to hold high expectations for them. High expectations are not just for kids at the "top." They are for all kids—no exceptions.

If you are truly dedicated to meeting the needs of the whole child, beginning with addressing their greatest needs, and if you are willing to figure out what their needs really are, you are showing that you genuinely care. At-risk students are yearning for at least one adult in their school to care about them; to build a relationship with them. When it comes to providing equity for all kids, we ought to start here.

REFLECT/CONNECT

Reflect: Do something kind for someone in need—I mean, really kind. How does it make you feel? What is it that prevents you from doing it again and again?

Are you wasting your energy and bludgeoning your psychological well-being on stupid stuff? What are those stupid things? Can you jettison at least one?

Connect: Share your reflections and experiences with a community of courageous leaders just like you by using social media.

Chapter 16

It Only Takes One

We can, whenever and wherever we choose, successfully teach all children whose schooling is of interest to us. We already know more than we need in order to do this. Whether we do it must finally depend on how we feel about the fact that we haven't so far.

—Ron Edmunds

If you don't tell your story, someone else will. School divisions across the country began an earnest conversation about equity several years ago, and since then, there seems to be a general misunderstanding regarding what exactly we are trying to accomplish. Unfortunately, the misunderstanding seems to be perpetuated by those wanting to politicize the topic. This is very unfortunate and seems to be driven by either ignorance or dishonesty.

The mission surrounding the provision of equity is simple: We want to *ensure* that every kid, no matter their disability, race, gender, or socioeconomic condition, receives what they need in order to be successful. Period. If you somehow disagree with that, then we can assume you hate puppies. We can argue about *how* to provide equity within our educational programs, but the concept of giving kids what they need and when and how they need it should not be the subject for debate. How could it?

Every school division has a mission statement, surely created through an excruciating and painful process. Most include something like this: "Our mission is to provide an innovative learning community that is committed to developing creative, confident, and knowledgeable citizens who are globally competitive and able to realize their potential as learners."

Right now, this commitment is not being realized for every student and, typically, the students left out are those of color, disadvantaged, LGBTQ+, and the disabled. They are not receiving everything they need in order to be successful. Forced busing, the ADA, IDEA, the A Nation at Risk study, high-stakes standardized testing, and No Child Left Behind have all failed to close the major achievement discrepancies.

So what do we do? First, we need to own this reality as school leaders. We can keep doing as we have been and, as Einstein described as the definition of insanity, "expect a different result." Or we can work differently and equip every teacher and staff member with the essential tools they need to help every kid become the absolute best version of themselves.

Second, we must choose to work differently. We must choose to reach all kids, encourage all kids, support all kids, and, ultimately, make connections with kids who, perhaps, we have not been able to connect with to this point. If we do not, many of these kids will continue to fall through the cracks and enter our community as young adults who are vulnerable, marginalized, aimless, and desperate for a chance. We can't allow this to happen, and we must put people in front of them who are sufficiently equipped to *help* them.

Our decision to work differently has paid off in my current school division. We continue to have one of the highest graduation rates in the state (96.2 percent overall for the class of 2021 and 95.5 percent for African American

Cause I Ain't Got a Pencil

by Joshua T. Dickerson

I woke myself up
Because we ain't got an alarm clock
Dug in the dirty clothes basket,
Cause ain't nobody washed my uniform
Brushed my hair and teeth in the dark,
Cause the lights ain't on
Even got my baby sister ready,
Cause my mama wasn't home.
Got us both to school on time,
To eat us a good breakfast.
Then when I got to class the teacher fussed
Cause I ain't got a pencil.

Figure 16.1. Cause I ain't got a pencil

students). But we still have gaps in places, and we need to continue to work to ensure that every kid receives what they need in order to be successful.

When we stereotype those low-achieving, impoverished, and often disabled students, we are only succeeding at placing yet another obstacle in their paths. Likewise, pushing them through our systems is just as irresponsible. If we consistently establish low expectations for them, they will meet them every time. Sometimes, it only took one individual—a teacher, a coach, a staff member—to look a kid in the eye and say, "I believe in you. You can accomplish anything you like. Don't let anyone tell you otherwise." These are the kinds of unsung heroes who can and do change kids' lives every day.

We can ensure that every kid receives what they need to be successful. You need to believe this with every ounce of your being, and, if we work together, we'll get there. The knife of influence, however, cuts both ways as explained by Mr. Bruce Springsteen.

ANOTHER REASON TO LOVE "THE BOSS"

Sharing that you are a Bruce Springsteen fan is like saying you like tacos. It seems like almost everyone does, and here is one more reason to love him.

On a recent podcast, Bruce Springsteen was talking about what drives him, what motivates him, and why he continues to tour. If you've seen him perform, you understand the motivation behind the question. He is an amazing entertainer. He plays for hours. He has boundless energy and engages with his audience with sincerity and vulnerability. His answer to the question was profound beyond words:

> A lot of us grew up with two kinds of people in our lives. On one hand we had someone close to us tell us that we were no good. That we'll never amount to anything. That we're worthless. But there is another person who tells us that we can do no wrong. That we are a gift from God. That we are perfect. What happens to a lot of people is they spend the rest of their lives trying to prove one of the people wrong and one of the people right.

Wow. What an amazing message. Can you relate? Can you see the faces of those two people from your childhood/adolescence? Those memories may stir up some really awful and really beautiful memories simultaneously.

As teachers, custodians, guidance counselors, food service workers, and administrators, we have an opportunity every day to be that person. The person whom someone else will want to look up to, to be like, and to make proud. We have that opportunity each day, but it is up to us to decide whether or not we want to shoulder that responsibility.

Reflect/Connect

Reflect: Start today to work differently and equip every teacher and staff member with the essential tools they need to help every kid become the absolute best version of themselves. Identify just one thing (material or training). Example: I hand out a laminated card with the "Cause I Ain't Got a Pencil" message to my new teachers each year.

Connect: Share your reflections and experiences with a community of courageous leaders just like you by using social media.

Chapter 17

Out of the Mouths of Babes

There's so much positivity in the world and your day-to-day life that to go as far as to say that you hate something or you wish it didn't exist and all the bad things in the world happen to you and only you, it's a joke. It's not real to have that much hate in your heart.

—Chance the Rapper

School leaders who lose their connection with students are doomed. The larger the school division or school, the more likely it is for leaders to miss those amazing and rewarding chances to spend time with students. It is a genuine and serious problem, but one that can be avoided if you are intentional about staying connected.

Please, create opportunities to spend time with students: create student advisory groups, eat lunch with them, attend their ball games, plays, and concerts. Wander out to the softball field during PE and hit a few. Attend club meetings and poetry readings. It matters . . . and it helps you and them. Remind yourself why you got into this business in the first place, because the hierarchy of fulfillment and joy remains intact: the kids are why we do what we do.

THE CURRENT GENERATION

We all get hit with the negative every single day. It is constant and relentless, but our response should be simple: Stay upbeat. Stay positive but confront the stuff that needs confronting. It seems that, for the current generation of students, a positive message resonates and influences accordingly.

Unfortunately, the world has plenty of bad folks who prefer it that way because they are unhappy, negative, and, even worse, anxious to receive attention by sharing a rotten message. But there is plenty of beauty in this world, plenty of positivity, and plenty of joy and hope. This generation seems to understand this, which should comfort all of us.

A local superintendent hosted a podcast recently that included a group of high school students. The students were asked about their culture, what they valued, how they viewed diversity, what we as adults can do better in order to help them. The answers were a timely and encouraging reminder that our nation is in good hands moving forward.

At the end of the podcast, the students were asked what he could do to be a better, more effective superintendent. A few students responded with "Keep doing stuff like this" and "Keep talking to us." Pretty simple stuff, really. They long for our attention, our encouragement, and our approval. So, we ought to give it to them.

This generation of students is going to change the world. They accept people who don't look, worship, learn, or live like they do. It seems they have a much better understanding of the needs of others and the importance of kindness and understanding than most adults. These kids get it, so listen to them. Commit to redoubling your efforts to listen and engage with students.

REFLECT/CONNECT

Reflect: Make a point to engage consistently with at least three students you've never spoken to before. After giving it a few weeks, how do you feel? How do they seem to feel? How does building relationships with students affect other areas of their school experience?

Connect: Share your reflections and experiences with a community of courageous leaders just like you by using social media.

Chapter 18

Three Letters from Teddy

This is a fictional story authored by Elizabeth Silance Ballard. It's tempting and somewhat comforting to believe that it is true, but it is not. It is, however, a motivating and uplifting message that any educator—past, present, or future—can relate to.

Each September, Miss Thompson greeted her new students with the words, "Boys & girls, I love you all the same. I have no favorites." Of course, she wasn't being completely truthful. Teachers do have favorites, and what is worse, they sometimes have students they just don't like.

Teddy Stallard was a boy Miss Thompson just didn't like, and for good reason. He was a sullen boy who sat slouched in his seat with his head down. When she spoke to him, he always answered in monosyllables of "yes" and "no." His clothes were musty and his hair unkempt. He was an unattractive boy in just about every way.

Whenever she marked Teddy's papers she got a certain perverse delight out of putting Xs next to the wrong answers. And when she put the "F" at the top of his papers, she always did it with a flair. She should have known better. Teachers have records, and she had records on Teddy:

First grade: Teddy shows promise with his work and attitude, but poor home situation.

Second grade: Teddy is a good boy, but he is too serious for a second grader. His mother is terminally ill.

Third grade: Teddy is becoming withdrawn and detached. His mother died this year. His father shows no interest.

Fourth grade: Teddy is a troubled child. He needs help.

Christmas came. The children brought presents to Miss Thompson and piled them on her desk. They crowded around to watch her open them. All the presents were wrapped in brightly colored paper, except for Teddy's present. His was wrapped in brown paper and held together with Scotch Tape. But to tell the truth, she was surprised that he even brought a present.

When she tore open the paper, out fell a rhinestone bracelet with most of the stones missing and an almost-empty bottle of cheap perfume. The other children giggled at the shabby gifts, but Miss Thompson had enough sense to snap on the bracelet and take some perfume out of the almost-empty bottle and put it on her wrist. Holding her wrist up to the other children she said, "Isn't it lovely?" The other children, taking their cue from the teacher, all agreed.

At the end of the day when all the other children had left, Teddy came over to her desk and said softly, "Miss Thompson, all day today you smelled just like my mother used to smell. That's her bracelet you're wearing. It looks very nice on you. I'm really glad you like my presents." After he left, she got down on her knees and buried her head in her hands and cried and cried and cried, and she asked God to forgive her.

The next day when the children came to class, they had a new teacher. It was still Miss Thompson, but she was a new teacher. She cared in ways that the old teacher didn't. She reached out in ways that the old teacher didn't. She reached out to all the children but especially to Teddy. She nurtured him and encouraged him and tutored him when he needed extra help. By the end of that school year Teddy had caught up with a lot of children. He was even ahead of some.

Teddy moved away and Miss Thompson didn't hear from him for a long time. Then, one day, seemingly out of nowhere, came a note:

Dear Miss Thompson, I'm graduating from high school. I wanted you to be the first to know. Love, Teddy Stallard

There was no address. But four years later there was another short note, and it read:

Dear Miss Thompson, I wanted you to be the first to know. I'm second in my class. The university has not been easy, but I really liked it. Love, Teddy Stallard

And four years later there was still another note:

Dear Miss Thompson, As of today I am Theodore J. Stallard, MD! How about that! I wanted you to be the first to know. I'm going to be married, the 27th of July to be exact. I want you to come and I want you to sit where my mother would have sat. You're the only family I have now. Dad died last year. Love, Teddy Stallard

And she went. And she sat where Teddy's mother would have sat because she deserved to be there. She was a teacher who had done something great for the Kingdom of God, and she deserved her reward.

This story has never lost its beauty and influence. It has been shared for decades with new teachers because it is so powerful and, more importantly, so accurate. Teachers do have favorites, which is normal, but the kids shouldn't know it.

Remember to share this with your teachers and constantly remind yourself that you are not in a race. Everything will get done. What you should be focused on during the first weeks of school, for example, is getting to know the kids. What do they like to eat? Do they have a favorite pet? What do they want to be when they grow up? Do they have brothers and sisters? Who is their hero? It's important—very important.

Students will make up their minds very quickly whether or not you really care about them. Don't blow this opportunity. Listen to kids carefully. Ask for feedback. It doesn't take that long, and it will pay off in dividends.

The old, and hopefully defunct, rule of thumb, the rule every experienced educator seemed eager to share, was "don't smile before Christmas." Perhaps during the last generation and before, this advice had merit. Back then, students were motivated by three things: fear of getting in trouble at school, which translated into getting in trouble at home; earning good grades; and the learning of new information. This is no longer the case, especially for at-risk students. What they do respond to are the teachers who they know truly care about them, who have taken the time to get to know them. These are the folks who are able to reach our neediest kids.

REFLECT/CONNECT

Reflect: At-risk students respond to those teachers whom they know truly care about them, who have taken the time to get to know them. These folks are able to reach our neediest kids, and we'd be in big trouble if we didn't have them. They make school meaningful and worth attending. Recognize these teachers. Use them as mentors for new teachers no matter how much experience they have.

Connect: Share your reflections and experiences with a community of courageous leaders just like you by using social media.

SECTION FOUR

Social Media, Email, and the Importance of Feeling Good

We all need to feel good about ourselves and about the work we do. It is important work. The kids we teach are important, and when we feel good, they might feel good also.

Chapter 19

Social Media

A Love-Hate Story

Social media is something of a double-edged sword. At its best, social media offers unprecedented opportunities for marginalized people to speak and bring much needed attention to the issues they face. At its worst, social media also offers "everyone" an unprecedented opportunity to share in collective outrage without reflection.

—Roxane Gay

The speed at which information is spread via social media has presented enormous problems for school divisions and school leaders. It is truly impossible to stay ahead of it, and once information is out there, it's out there for good. It seems that *after* each school shooting, investigators discover social media posts and pictures that *should* have raised red flags . . . but apparently didn't.

In terms of schools, all of us would welcome staff whose sole responsibility it is to monitor social media looking for nefarious activity, but most don't have that luxury, and in some respects it wouldn't matter anyway. Once the send button is hit it can't be reversed.

A great example of the "double-edged" nature of social media involve threats against schools and individuals that ultimately find their way to school leadership. It is a positive thing that people are willing to share the threats they read, but a negative thing that threats can be so easily sent, and often sent again (e.g., retweeting). This is an ongoing headache that doesn't seem to want to go away. Perhaps social media will eventually burn out and give way to a different communication resource, or maybe people will universally tire of it. Unlikely, but we can dream, can't we?

Obviously, we need to use social media to our advantage, and we need to use it appropriately. Here's a solid rule of thumb: don't write or share anything that you wouldn't say or share in person, face-to-face. Here's a second good guidepost: verify, verify, verify. The amount of misinformation flowing from social media is staggering and disturbing and often impossible to rein in. This is yet another reason why, as school leaders, we've got to keep telling our story clearly, factually, and transparently.

Although it is wise to carefully choose your battles, that does not mean that we ignore the inaccurate information that is damaging and intended to harm. We have to fight some of those battles by simply providing the correct information, and social media is a fine way to accomplish this.

REFLECT/CONNECT

Reflect: In what ways can you harness the positive power of social media? When someone posts inaccurate information about your school/school

"I just feel fortunate to live in a world with so much disinformation at my fingertips."

Figure 19.1. I just feel fortunate. Used with permission. © P. C. Vey, www.CartoonStock. com

system, how can you respond in a way that sets the story straight while not fanning the flames of confrontation?

Connect: Share your reflections and experiences with a community of courageous leaders just like you by using social media.

Chapter 20

That Special Thing

I think the headline [of *Sully*] should be, "Good news wins." We're obsessed with bad news. . . . These channels only make money by keeping the public terrified. So we're guaranteed to have an endless supply of bad news. . . . We're being coached on how to feel poorly, and we need to look at the light.

—Todd Komarnicki, writer of the screenplay *Sully*

You just have to find that thing that's special about you that distinguishes you from all the others, and through true talent, hard work, and passion, anything can happen.

—Dr. Dre

Todd Komarnicki is, well, kind of famous, but you would never, ever know it from meeting him. He is genuinely humble and beyond comfortable in his own skin. Todd is a man of infinite talent and work ethic. His faith and gentle spirit are a model for all leaders to follow. Todd loves to help kids. He has the heart of a servant and is in a constant state of motion when it comes to nurturing, encouraging, and teaching. During a recent interview, Todd was asked what advice he might give to students aspiring to become writers. Here is what he said:

Writing is work. It's eight to ten hours every day, just writing. But here's the thing. I never want to write. I never wake up and think, I can't wait to write today! It's hard work, but the payoff and satisfaction that can come from having written—that is worth all the effort and in the end it is vital to remember that writing isn't about desire. It is about discipline, and discipline just means to be a disciple, to follow, to follow your calling, so if you feel it burning inside of you that you need to write but don't want to, that's okay.

Just follow the calling, and the blank page will get filled up with beauty word by word.

So, great writers like Todd don't just sit down and allow the words to flow like honey from their imaginations with little effort, or struggle, or procrastination? His message is such a valuable lesson for our kids and for all of us, really. Hard work is hard, raising and teaching kids is hard, but the rewards of our efforts include feelings of satisfaction and accomplishment that you can't get anywhere else. The belief that you have something valuable to offer others comes from a belief in oneself, a belief that evolves through hard work, sacrifice, and, yes, bravery.

We live in a society that wants immediate success and reward, but life does not work that way, and finding that "thing" that we are willing to dedicate our blood, sweat, and tears to is very tricky and very elusive. Helping students discover and realize their talents can happen through simple things like encouragement or a positive observation, or maybe even a phone call home.

Some find their talent very early in life, and some find it closer to the end. For some it's fairly obvious. For others, it's found only after spending years engaged in something, some occupation or career path that is completely unrewarding but puts bread on the table and pays the rent.

Some never find it, which is the greatest tragedy of all.

Some know exactly what their talent is but eventually have it wrung out of them by a culture that prefers punishing errors and ridiculing differences while naively expecting allegiance to a familiar path with conventional (and typically low) expectations.

But we all have at least one exceptional talent. Helping kids find and enhance theirs is one of our most critically important challenges. Unfortunately, the traditional educational model, one that is based on the factory system developed during the American Industrial Revolution, has made the task more difficult, and we end up with an instructional system and/or model that actually works against kids finding and sculpting their talent(s). They've all got them. Perhaps you will be the first person to see it in some of your students. Wouldn't that be something?

REFLECT/CONNECT

Reflect: In order for people of any age to find their talent, they need opportunities to explore, experience, and learn about themselves. How can you encourage these things? How can we provide these opportunities?

Connect: Share your reflections and experiences with a community of courageous leaders just like you by using social media.

Chapter 21

This Is for Those Who Hate Email

Most of us receive a ton of email, the majority of it general in nature: people asking good questions, sharing necessary information, saying hello, or trying to sell something. However, we've grown accustomed to email communication that doesn't fit into any of the aforementioned categories. This list of one-off email types is just for fun but is sure to resonate. We'll call them "The Six Most Frequent Email Types School Leaders Receive."

The "Mr. and/or Ms. Jim Beam" email: usually received sometime between 9:30 p.m. and 2:00 a.m. Lots of threats, profanity, and misspellings, for example, "That principle is a jackass!" These emails are fairly easy to identify, especially if received over the weekend. My all-time favorite started this way: "I was standing in line at the ABC store today and heard . . ." If you want to get the attention of the superintendent, that opener will work every time.

The "Perry Mason Jr." email: usually includes a threat to sue and always includes a whole bunch of question marks. These emails often come from a person who works in a lawyer's office, is perhaps a paralegal (lawyers, themselves, usually never send emails), maybe took a law class in college, is related to a lawyer, or thinks they are qualified to interpret the law because they were sued once. Not sure what percentage of those who threaten to sue us actually do, but it is certainly miniscule.

The "Super Sleuth" email: anonymous, typically sent from a fictitious account (but not always, which is hilarious). These emails are often reporting the perceived misdeeds of others or are simply telling you that you suck. Many include statements like, "I'm sending this anonymously because I don't want my child to experience repercussions." Ugh.

The "Mission Impossible" email: includes requests that are impossible to approve or are completely impractical/inequitable. Example: "My child really needs a one-on-one aide for the rest of his life, someone who can provide occasional foot massages."

The "I read it on Facebook" email: the worst of them all. Trying to put the rumor-toothpaste back into the tube-of-truth is impossible once it's hit

99

social media. No matter how preposterous the rumor is, plenty of people will believe what they read on social media, with Facebook topping them all.

The *War and Peace* email: so long that there is no way you're going to read the entire thing, no matter what the topic is. They often end with something like, "I look forward to your reply" or "I expect answers to all of my questions ASAP" What ever happened to picking up the phone?

The simple truth is that people will write in an email what they would never say to your face. Don't be like them. If you write an email while angry or frustrated, step away and revisit it in a couple of hours. You will be glad you did.

REFLECT/CONNECT

Reflect: What are some of the emails you have received that fit into the categories listed in this chapter? What new categories do you have to create for other ones?

Connect: Share your reflections and experiences with a community of courageous leaders just like you by using social media.

Chapter 22

Just Stop Complaining

Everyone makes choices in life. Some bad, some good. It's called living, and if you want to bow out, then go right ahead. But don't do it halfway. Don't linger in whiner's limbo.

—Maria V. Snyder

We can complain because rose bushes have thorns, or rejoice because thorn bushes have roses.

—Abraham Lincoln

What we need to do is always lean into the future; when the world changes around you and when it changes against you—what used to be a tail wind is now a head wind—you have to lean into that and figure out what to do because complaining isn't a strategy.

—Jeff Bezos

Don't be a complainer. Model patience, understanding, positivity, grace, and forgiveness and it will rub off on the people you lead. People who expect positive things to happen and believe that people are basically good typically get the result they anticipate. The same is true for those who expect negative things to happen and think the worst of people. They get what they predict.

Ultimately, it comes down to your attitude and what lens you are looking through. Charles Swindoll has this to say about attitude:

ATTITUDES

The longer I live, the more I realize the importance
of choosing the right attitude in life.
Attitude is more important than facts.
It is more important than your past;
more important than your education or your financial situation;
more important than your circumstances, your successes, or your failures;
more important than what other people think or say or do.
It is more important than your appearance, your giftedness, or your skills.
It will make or break a company. It will cause a church to soar or sink.
It will make the difference between a happy home or a miserable home.
You have a choice each day regarding the attitude you will embrace.
Life is like a violin.
You can focus on the broken strings that dangle,
or you can play your life's melody on the one that remains.
You cannot change the years that have passed,
nor can you change the daily tick of the clock.
You cannot change the pace of your march toward your death.
You cannot change the decisions or reactions of other people.
And you certainly cannot change the inevitable.
Those are strings that dangle!
What you *can* do is play on the one string that remains—your attitude.
I am convinced that life is 10 percent what happens to me
and 90 percent how I react to it.
The same is true for you.

Chuck Swindoll Copyright © 1981, 1982 by Charles R. Swindoll, Inc. All
rights reserved worldwide. Used by permission.

There's an "organization" in our community called CAVE: Citizens Against
Virtually Everything. You probably have the same one. It is a powerful and
consistent organization but one that leaders should never belong to.

Its members are folks who believe that the provision of equity for all students is somehow shrouded in conspiracy. Surely providing for the needs of
all kids must have some evil motive.

Those who have tried to link critical race theory (CRT) with the goal of
lifting up the kids (providing an equitable education) who have consistently
struggled not only don't understand how equity differs from equality, but
they also don't understand CRT. It's a theory, not a curriculum and not an
instructional method. Attempts to construct a relationship between the two
are theatrics designed to frighten and confuse people . . . and win elections.

CRT is a framework that involves inherent bias within many social constructs and "a collection of critical stances against the existing *legal order* from a race-based point of view." The other, equity in an educational setting, begins with getting to know and understand our kids, figuring out what their needs are, and then providing for those needs. That's it.

Sometimes it is important for us to respond publicly to those who are anxious to tell our story for us. Not-so-informed stakeholders can do damage that is otherwise impossible to repair. Those who attempt to shift the narrative to suit their own desire for attention, or who are simply angry, unhappy people, sometimes need to be corrected publicly.

Fire sometimes needs to be fought with fire. Listen, if we don't tell our story someone else will, and probably not very well. Prior to the last few years, this may not have been the best approach to dealing with misinformation, but we are in a new place. We are under attack by many who would be happy to see public education fail in this country in favor of a different system. We've got to fight back: wisely, specifically, articulately, and consistently. Don't expect others to do the fighting for us.

When it comes to telling your school's story, make the positive so loud that the negative is impossible to hear. Parents can and should play a vital role in spreading a message of positivity and excellence to the greater community, but they will only do if they genuinely believe it's happening. It is our job to lead them to a place where they believe in you, your school, your teachers, and your staff.

SUMMARY

Don't let people tell your story. Don't let them hijack your narrative. But, if they do, you may need to take action. One of the greatest mistakes we as educational leaders have made over the past few years (the COVID-19 years) is remaining on the defensive and being reluctant to go on the offensive. The fact is that we have done a fantastic job in spite of tremendous hardships and obstacles. We can say it. We can point to the successes we have achieved. We can push back at the folks who have suddenly become educational experts and who are anxious to throw stones at something they know very little about.

Going to school does not make anyone an expert in school. *We* are the experts. *We* have earned that distinction because we are here, and we are doing the work and doing it very well. Don't be ashamed to share that.

REFLECT/CONNECT

Reflect: When someone tries to hijack your story, correct them. Perhaps even publicly. Don't let them get away with it. This is risky, I know, but we've been back on our heels for far too long. It's time for us to tell our own story.

Connect: Share your reflections and experiences with a community of courageous leaders just like you by using social media.

Chapter 23

Because No One Else Will

I don't want to live in the kind of world where we don't look out for each other. Not just the people that are close to us, but anybody who needs a helping hand. I can't change the way anybody else thinks, or what they choose to do, but I can do my bit.

—Charles de Lint

When I do good, I feel good. When I do bad, I feel bad. That is my religion.

—Abraham Lincoln

Mary Jones, a newly remarried mother of seven children, had just moved into a sprawling new community in Southern California called "Friendly Hills." It's one of those communities not close to anything other than a couple of schools and a golf course; otherwise, nothing was really within walking distance. One day, Mary left her home in her new red Cadillac with her youngest son in the back seat. She had only driven a few blocks when both Mary and her son saw something they had never seen before in their neighborhood: two young Black men. They were standing next to an old beat-up car, hood raised, smoke billowing. One of the men had extended his thumb in the hopes of hitching a ride. There were no Black families in Friendly Hills and in the adjacent town.

Mrs. Jones then did something very surprising: She stopped and offered to help. It was surprising then, but in retrospect, also not surprising at all.

Mary Jones raised seven children essentially on her own with a lot of help from her oldest daughter, Patty. Mrs. Jones worked long hours as a waitress in a bowling alley. She was a single parent, tough, focused exclusively on providing for her kids. And she ran a very tight ship and was able to stretch every dollar in order to feed and clothe her family. Her kids often slept three to a room. Then everything changed. Mary married a local doctor whom she had frequently waited on at the bowling alley. He was a good tipper, so she kept an eye out for him as he often came with friends to bowl, play pool, and have a few beers. They married, and he took on the shared responsibility of raising their seven children. They moved into a beautiful new home, the children all got bikes, Mary got a new car, and their lives changed completely.

The two young Black men were clearly relieved. They hopped in the car and one of the guys immediately began to explain their situation: they had gotten off the freeway and become hopelessly lost. This was before cell phone and GPS, so getting lost was not unusual. He explained that they had been driving around for some time, and their car finally gave out. They asked Mary if she could take them to the nearest pay phone, and she happily agreed. They were relieved and began to smile broadly. They were so grateful.

Many years later, as Mary sat on her patio with her youngest son, he asked her if she remembered that day. She shot back, "Of course I remember. I remember it quite well." He asked her why, why she, a young woman with a small boy in tow in a brand-new car, had stopped to help these men. Wasn't she afraid? She again shot back, "Of course not." He dug a bit deeper: Why had she done it? Why did she stop? "Because if I hadn't stopped to help them," she explained, "no one else would have."

We had changed homes, we had all of our material needs met, and Mary could finally breathe a bit easier, but she never forgot where she came from, what she had endured, and what it was like to need help desperately and not always get it. She saw those guys not as threats but as two human beings who needed help, and she was able to provide it.

As educators, we are called to serve everyone who walks into our classrooms. It doesn't matter what they look like, where they come from, what their past transgressions are, or what other teachers or administrators might say about them. We are put on this earth to help them, and, in some instances, if we don't help them, no one else will. *That* is how important our jobs are.

The time we spend preparing for and pursuing our careers is short. Our time with our friends and colleagues is short, and our time with our families is exceedingly precious and short. We know these things to be true, and we repeat them with conviction, but the distractions of life, which are typically petty and unimportant, can often elbow out the important stuff, like helping those who need it the most.

The Lincoln quote at the beginning of this chapter is simply yet profound. Life is short. Do good because, when you do, you'll feel better. Others will feel better also. Your actions have a ripple affect among the people you live and work with. Life is too short to feel bad about much of anything. Some things can't be helped. We don't always have control over them, but we do have control over ourselves and our attitudes. What good does it do for a person to go through life feeling bad? Do good and you will feel better and so will the people around you.

Lincoln endured unfathomable hardship and great loss, but he was always kind and forgiving. He invited political enemies to serve on his staff, and he understood that kindness of spirit was not just intended for friends. It was intended for all.

One final thought on this subject: we *all* have the power to make the lives of those around us better if we are *willing* to do so. Perhaps no one knows what battles you fight, and you don't know what battles the people who come into contact with are fighting, but we all fight them, sometimes daily. Sometimes the battles are practical and obvious: My car broke down, I am lost, and there is no one around here who will help me. But sometimes they are complex and concealed: no one cares about me, and I have no one to talk to about my feelings or my struggles.

We have the power to help those with the obvious needs, and we also have the power to help with the conspicuous needs. What it comes down to, as Edmonds suggests, is "how we feel about" the fact that we haven't done all that we can do to help.

REFLECT/CONNECT

Reflect: We have control over ourselves and our attitudes. If your attitude needs adjusting, go ahead and adjust it.

Is there someone you work with whose life you can make better? Perhaps a little easier? Is there something preventing you from doing just that?

Connect: Share your reflections and experiences with a community of courageous leaders just like you by using social media.

Chapter 24

Tragedy Is Tragic No Matter Who You Are

The heart is our hidden center, beyond the grasp of our reason and of others; only the Spirit of God can fathom the human heart and know it fully. The heart is the place of decision, deeper than our psychic drives. It is the place of truth, where we choose life or death. It is the place of encounter.

—Pope John Paul II

We are in the life-saving business. Every day you are saving lives, literally. You must not ever forget that.

—Lorraine Monroe

Losers are people who are so afraid of not winning,
   they don't even try.

—Grandpa, *Little Miss Sunshine*

Decisions that can, ultimately, impact people's health and well-being are incredibly hard to make. No one who has ever been in such a position will ever understand just how wrenching it can be. As young educators, we could have never imagined how the decisions we make as leaders will and do impact people so profoundly and so directly . . . but we still have to make them.

If you are a person of faith, you may believe that God put you in a place of leadership because He knows that you are ready. That you will make a difference, and that you are the right person for the job. That is quite a challenge, but whether you are a person of faith or not, the ultimate challenge in regard to decision-making begins with making choices that don't intentionally harm anyone, that keep kids safe, and that generate trust among parents and staff.

They will trust your decisions because, ultimately, those decisions mean that everyone arrives home safely after school. In short, student and staff safety come first.

Life is precious. Steps to preserve it are beyond essential. Showing honor and respect for *all* lives is paramount. When individuals spout off statistics about the number of deaths due to COVID-19 versus the "ordinary" flu or about how just as many die from car accidents or from violence in order to make a point politically, it feels obtuse, callous, and uncaring. It doesn't feel right because it's not right, and there is a risk that our kids are being indoctrinated into viewing some loss of life as less important than other loss of life.

We live in a society that, unfortunately, has forgotten just how precious life is. Every unnecessary death is the loss of someone's child, parent, sibling, or friend. If you've experienced the loss of a loved one or dealt with the trauma associated with the loss of life, you understand. Keeping kids safe in school is our number one priority, but schools need help. They cannot do it on their own.

TIFFANY

About a month or so into his first principalship, a student died in one of his school's classrooms. It happened early one fall morning, quiet, a very typical start to the school day. Eric was startled by two girls frantically running in his direction, pleading with him to come to their classroom. They said, "Tiffany passed out. We can't wake her up." Eric had many experiences over the years with students passing out, so although he ran to the classroom, he wasn't that concerned—until he entered the room. He saw fifteen-year-old Tiffany still at her desk, stiff, pale, eyes wide open. He knew she was gone.

Eric cleared the classroom and radioed for help and, although he and others provided CPR until an ambulance arrived, there was nothing any of them could do. He called his superintendent and drove to the hospital. Tiffany was pronounced dead shortly after he arrived. Her family had been placed in a room off to one side of the emergency room. When the doctor entered that room and shared the news with her family, the screams and cries Eric heard remain with him to this day.

That morning haunts Eric regularly twenty-three years later. It will never leave him. Tiffany was sent to school that morning by her mother and uncle expecting that she would be taken take care of, that her well-being would be insured. Learning later that Tiffany had a congestive heart ailment and that her family knew that she could go at any time was and is of little comfort. She died in Eric's school, under his watch, and he will live with that forever.

Our students are so precious, and this is part of our burden as school leaders: keeping kids safe and ignoring those who question our attempts to make schools safer places.

SANCTITY OF LIFE

In 1991, Dr. Lorraine Monroe founded the Frederick Douglass Academy, a public school in New York City's Harlem, with the belief that caring instructors, a disciplined but creative environment, and a refusal to accept mediocrity could transform the lives of inner-city kids. Her experiment was a huge success. Today, the academy is one of the finest schools in the country, sending graduates to Ivy League colleges and registering the third-highest SAT scores in New York City.

The reason that people like Dr. Monroe have been so successful working with kids who, frankly, others would rather not work with is because they truly believe that they are saving lives, and that each life matters. This is the attitude and belief system we must have in our schools, but it can be heartbreaking work and so damn difficult. This is another reason for the recent teacher shortage and exit of so many great educators. They recognize the value of their work. They worry about their kids and feel tremendous guilt when they cannot provide for them what they know they need.

COVID-19 has exacerbated the trauma that teachers feel when students struggle. People generally don't get this, and some of the ignorance and stupidity that has surfaced regarding the value of our teachers has driven them away.

A LOSING MENTALITY

Elsewhere in this book there is a reference to a very well-known national figure who referred to teachers as "losers" during the 2020 presidential campaign. Here is the exact quote:

> You don't have to be indoctrinated by these loser teachers that are trying to sell you on socialism from birth. You don't have to do it. Because you can think for yourselves. They can't.

This is the kind of sentiment and attitude among some very influential national figures that educators are up against. It is certainly not pervasive, but it exists. People who know nothing about what teachers do every day throwing stones in order to rile up a crowd is absolutely pathetic. Certainly, many of the teachers this gentleman ever had are ashamed to be in any way associated with him. He owes every one of them an apology.

The preceding quote was a targeted rant intended to encourage all educators to push back—hard. We don't have to endure this sort of treatment silently.

If we have learned anything over the past two years it's that we have become the targets of people who have lost the argument and don't know what to do next. These people have learned that we (teachers, school boards, principals, and superintendents) will often sit silently and allow others to hijack the narrative, even though their narrative is often wrong. Look no further than the previous quote. "Sell you socialism from birth?" Teachers barely have time to teach the adopted curriculum and use the restroom. Name-calling, dishonesty, and disrespect: That is what a true loser looks like. But that is not what this chapter is about. It's about real winners, real experiences, and real risk-taking.

Winners build up, and losers tear down. Those educators who care, who genuinely consider the needs of others before their own, will be successful and will become our future leaders. They will take risks because they have courage, and they recognize that standing still is really moving backward. They are selfless and humble, and they do what they do not because they want praise and attention, but because they care.

Someone once said that the true measure of a man is what he gives to those who can give nothing in return. This is perhaps the truest definition of what school leadership should be all about.

Reflect/Connect

Reflect: Do you have a personal mantra that you repeat often and try to live by? What is it? Is it on your email tagline or business card? Such small but important reminders benefit you directly.

Connect: Share your reflections and experiences with a community of courageous leaders just like you by using social media.

Chapter 25

Pivoting, Going on the Offensive, and Growing Up

Technology is something you have to embrace because technology is part of our generation. Digital natives, for instance, are people who grew up in a world that always had the Internet and who always had smartphones. Millennials aren't too far behind: my generation of people, who were in the mix of the Internet when it first came out.

—Jon Batiste

The very first thing I tell every intern on the first day is that their internship exists solely on their resume. As far as I am concerned, they are a full-time member of my team. For all the negative stereotypes about millennials, you would be astounded by how hard they work when they believe their contribution matters.

—Jay Samit

For educators, the words *nasal swab*, *hybrid instruction*, *asynchronous learning*, and *learning loss* will forever be associated with the COVID-19 pandemic. It seems we all learned a new language since the virus hit, not because we wanted to but because we didn't have a choice. We have all grown to really dislike these pandemic-associated words but not nearly as much as we've disliked the word that we now associate with moving out of our comfort zones and asking even more of people who are hanging by a thread: *pivot*.

Let's face it, baby boomers and Gen Xers have one thing in common when it comes to the expectations that have been heaped upon them recently: they often don't pivot very well. Millennials and Generation Zers are much better at it than we are. When required to pivot, we get very uncomfortable, even panicked. Also frustrating for educators is the fact that our school parents don't like pivoting either.

Changing direction suddenly and overtly are not things we are accustomed to doing, but we've had to do it a lot and often with little warning. Initial fears often sprouted from our ignorance surrounding the meaningful and purposeful use of technology. Millennials grew up with technology, the internet, and social media. Although we preferred to hang on to our BlackBerry smartphones for as long as possible, millennials wait in line patiently, sometimes for hours, to purchase the newest iPhone.

Change is a good thing for millennials, and they seem to embrace change just as fervently as we embrace familiarity. What we've seen happen in our school division over the past couple of years is millennials easily adjusting to systemic instructional change, including entirely new expectations regarding the use of technology for instruction. This was and is not necessarily the case for all millennials, nor have all boomers and Gen Xers struggled. Many have done just fine, adjusting comfortably and calmly in the midst of terrible pressure and unrealistic expectations.

Millennials and Gen Zers seem to possess a certain courage, awareness, acceptance, and (appropriate) social outrage that we others have not shown to the same extent.

We witnessed, and sometimes experienced, forced busing and the later stages and aftermath of desegregation, and we remember homosexuality and transgenderism being referred to as "abnormal," a "disease," and a "curse from God." Moreover, we remember a much more innocent time when kids and teachers in rural areas would hunt before school and leave their rifles in gun racks on the way in.

By contrast, millennials have witnessed George Floyd's murder, embraced the LBGQT+ movement, and accepted diversity in a way that many evangelicals have not in spite of what Christ commanded: Love thy neighbor.

Millennials have witnessed a horrifying and startling increase in the number of school shootings, and they wonder aloud why something other than "prayers for the families" hasn't been done in order to stop the murder of innocent children in places where they should feel absolutely safe, places where the last thing on earth they should have to worry about is being shot. They scratch their heads when people from previous generations scream at and threaten school board members about mask-wearing and vaccinations or legislation introduced to make it more difficult for individuals to purchase AK-47s. It doesn't make a whole lot of sense to the younger generation, and it shouldn't.

In some respects, what we just endured and grown through are changes and stretches that would have likely occurred over several years, accompanied by the predictable kicking and screaming each step of the way. We have certainly *talked* about the more fervent and pervasive use of technology for a long time, but frankly, the evolution did not occur as we had hoped as a result of it being too hard and too expensive.

We weren't ready for the change and transitioning from an instructional model that we have relied on for more than one hundred years had practically no sense of urgency attached to it. That all changed around February 2020.

If there is a blessing associated with COVID-19 and schools, it is the fact that we *had* to pivot, and quickly, despite insufficient training, insufficient technology, insufficient bandwidth, insufficient funding (at first), and sometimes insufficient leadership. We weren't afraid to lead or avoided leading; we just weren't sure how. We were all freaked and ill-prepared, but we pulled off a miracle in a relatively short period of time and under tremendous pressure.

Were the results perfect? No, not by a long shot. At times it was a complete disaster, but we got it done. It could be argued that it was our finest moment, a moment that took courage and tremendous resilience.

We should all be very proud of what we just accomplished. We should hold our heads high with a sense of great accomplishment. Unfortunately, we've been put on the defensive and stayed there rather than going on the offensive. The misguided and, frankly, batshit-crazy fixation on critical race theory (CRT) that is referenced elsewhere in this book was one of the subjects that put many of us back on our heels. People attempting to link incredibly important initiatives like instructional equity and social and emotional learning with CRT demonstrate their ignorance and, in some cases, their intellectual dishonesty.

What people, parents especially, are or were angry about is the fact that schools were closed for long stretches, virtual instruction was marginally successful, and kids experienced real learning loss. That is where the anger comes from, not CRT. If you pin down most of the people who have expressed paranoia and outrage regarding CRT, they likely won't be able to tell you exactly what it is or how it has manifested itself in our schools—because it hasn't.

TIME TO SAY, "ENOUGH!"

If you've watched what has happened in school board meetings across the country, then you have witnessed exactly what is meant by "being on the defensive." We've seen scores of outraged citizens losing their minds regarding masks, vaccinations, school closures, and CRT.

Have you noticed what school boards and school leadership have been doing during these same meetings? They have remained on the defensive.

Typical school board meeting decorum has traditionally kept leadership silently in a corner, but we don't have to stay there. Instigating confrontation is not the answer, even though in many instances that is precisely what these folks have been looking for. We can, however, take a position and advance it with confidence, energy, and evidence. We can rebuke people who don't know how to behave in meetings, and we can remind people that their kids are watching, that name-calling is a punishable offense in our schools, and that threats are the last resort of someone who has lost the argument.

It is completely appropriate to remind citizens that what we expect from kids in schools is a baseline standard for appropriate behavior in a public setting. In short, they need to grow up and show the kind of respect that they demand from us.

REFLECT/CONNECT

Reflect: Do you have a student advisory group? Or is there a system in place that allows students to communicate directly with you? If you don't have one, create one, but make sure it features them doing the talking and sharing their thoughts. Your role should be simply to lead the conversation.

Connect: Share your reflections and experiences with a community of courageous leaders just like you by using social media.

Chapter 26

One Final Message

Every day, think as you wake up, today I am fortunate to be alive, I have a precious human life, I am not going to waste it. I am going to use all my energies to develop myself, to expand my heart out to others; to achieve enlightenment for the benefit of all beings. I am going to have kind thoughts towards others, I am not going to get angry or think badly about others. I am going to benefit others as much as I can.

—the Dalai Lama

Imagine you are given the opportunity to speak directly to every school administrator in your school divisions, or state, or across the country one last time before leaving the world of K–12 public education. Even better, what if you had that opportunity to address them now? What would you say? Think about it. Everyone is listening, hanging on your every word. What is the message you'd share? It's pretty boring as far as fantasies are concerned, but the idea of sharing an uninhibited and honest message with people who are empowered to make lasting change should be incredibly exciting. Perhaps your message might sound something like this:

Whether we are willing to admit it or not, our schools have some dead people working in them. Some died a long time ago. Some passed away just recently. Some were never alive to begin with. I am talking about administrators, teachers, and staff members.

We need either to bring those people back to life or help them find new professions, ones that do not involve kids. This should not be optional, nor should any school division establish roadblocks that make it harder to take the necessary steps. We need to do our jobs, support our teachers and staff, and provide targeted assistance as needed. But, at the end of the day, we also need to demonstrate the courage to do what is right for our kids, to make very difficult choices, and to hold uncomfortable conversations. This is our job.

Each year, parents take their kids to local big box stores to purchase school supplies, cool new outfits, perhaps a brand-new backpack. The excitement is palpable. Back-to-school nights are exciting and energizing—then we place kids in schools with some people who are dead inside. They've lost it or, perhaps, never had it. The students end up paying the price. They have wildly different school experiences.

For many, the joy and excitement disappear after the first week. Why do we allow this to happen? Why do we subject our students to people who can't reach them, don't really care about them, and, worst of all, don't even like kids?

Here is the thing: we have the power and authority to do something about this very serious problem, and there are a plethora of resources at our fingertips!

Literally hundreds, perhaps thousands, of books, articles, and staff development plans have been written to help school admin help teachers and staff—*but none of it really matters unless we are courageous enough to take action, to confront the uncomfortable, to rock the boat, and even to admit that we need help and that we cannot do it alone.*

We've all heard it said that it takes a student three full years to overcome one year with a lousy teacher. It can be easily argued that it takes about the same amount of time for a school to recover from one year with a bad principal. Imagine the damage a lousy principal can do if allowed to remain in his or her position indefinitely. We should not be allowing this to happen. We owe it to our kids and our teachers.

I am comfortable laying this gauntlet down because it is truth. It takes courage and the conviction of *knowing* that what is best for kids is what is best, period. In the end, we all need to sleep well at night knowing that the criticism we absorbed, anxiety we felt, stress we endured, and gray hair we grew and then lost was all worth it because we helped kids become the best versions of themselves, and we did the same for our teachers.

Finally, let me repeat what each of you already know but sometimes forget: teaching is one of the most noble and honorable professions on the planet. We need to emphasize this fact with enthusiasm and consistency.

This is not the time to make teaching seem less attractive. We have the power to raise the importance of teaching in the minds of stakeholders, especially those talented and good-tempered people who feel called to teach and, perhaps, serve in school leadership roles.

Sort of a downer of a message but one that every current school leader needs to absorb, and every future school leader come to terms with before heading down that path. This is, perhaps, the most important human resource-related responsibility any of us has: placing kids with competent people who care about their jobs and their students.

Reflect/Connect

Reflect: Is there an educator who you suspect is not 100 percent committed to doing what's best for kids? Schedule a courageous conversation with them this week.

Connect: Share your reflections and experiences with a community of courageous leaders just like you by using social media.

Bibliography

Ashton, P. T., and R. B. Webb. *Making a Difference: Teachers' Sense of Efficacy and Student Achievement.* New York: Longman, 1966.

Bloom, B. S., and D. R. Krathwohl. *Taxonomy of Educational Objectives; The Classification of Educational Goals by a Committee of College and University Examiners. Handbook I: Cognitive Domain.* New York: Longmans, Green, 1956.

Bridgeland, John M., John J. DiIulio, and Karen Burke. *The Silent Epidemic: Perspectives of High School Dropouts.* A report by Civic Enterprises in association with Peter D. Hart Research Associates for the Bill & Melinda Gates Foundation. March 2006. https://docs.gatesfoundation.org/documents/thesilentepidemic3 -06final.pdf.

Broflowski, Jennifer. "The Evolving Online Test Prep Market." Howthemarketworks.com. 2020. https://education.howthemarketworks.com/the -evolving-online-test-prep-market/.

Cunningham, D., and S. A. Nogle. "Implementing a Semesterized Block Schedule: Six Key Elements." *High School Magazine* 3, no. 3 (1996): 29–33.

Dean, Cornelia. "When Science Suddenly Mattered, in Space and in Class." *New York Times* (September 25, 2007).

Dintersmith, Ted. *What School Could Be.* Princeton, NJ: Princeton University Press, 2018.

Federal Bureau of Investigation. "2020 NCIC Missing Person and Unidentified Person Statistics." https://www.fbi.gov/file-repository/2020-ncic-missing-person -and-unidentified-person-statistics.pdf/view.

Gardner, Howard. *Multiple Intelligences.* New York: Basic Books, 1993.

Hanson, Melanie. "College Graduation Statistics." Education Data Initiative. August 9, 2021. https://educationdata.org/number-of-college-graduates.

Hunt, Judith. "Make Room for Daddy . . . and Mommy: Helicopter Parents Are Here." *The Journal of Academic Administration in High Education* 4, no. 1 (2011): 9–11.

Isherwood, Stephen. In Institute of Student Employers, The Global Skills Gap in the 21st Century. London: QS Quacquarelli Symonds Ltd. Intelligence Unit. 2018. https://www.topuniversities.com/sites/default/files/qsglobalskillsgapreport.pdf.

Marzano, R. J. *A Theory-Based Meta-Analysis of Research on Instruction.* Aurora, CO: Mid-Continent Regional Educational Laboratory. 1998. http://www.mcrel.org/pdf/instruction/5982rr_instructionmeta_analysis.pdf.

Marzano, R. J., B. B. Gaddy, and C. Dean. *What Works in Classroom Instruction.* Aurora, CO: Mid-Continent Regional Educational Laboratory. 2000. http://www.mcrel.org/PDF/Instruction/5992TG_What_Works.pdf.

Marzano, Robert J., Pickering, Debra J., and Pollock, Jane E. *Classroom Instruction That Works: Research-Based Strategies for Increasing Student Achievement.* ASCD, 2001.

Meir, Deborah. "Educating a Democracy." *Boston Review.* February–March, 2000.

Meno, Chris. "Helicopter Parents Stir up Anxiety and Depression." Indiana University Newsroom. 2013. https://newsinfo.iu.edu/web/page/normal/6073.html.

New International Version. (2011). BibleGateway.com. http://www.biblegateway.com/versions/New-International-Version-NIV-Bible/#booklist.

Puiu, Tibi. "Your Smartphone Is Millions of Times More Powerful than the Apollo 11 Guidance Computers." *ZME Science* (May 13, 2021).

Robinson, Ted. "Changing Education Paradigms." RSA ANIMATE on YouTube. 2010. https://www.ted.com/talks/sir_ken_robinson_changing_education_paradigms.

Slekar, Tim. "Educator: There's A Mass Teacher Exodus, Not Shortage." Interview conducted by Mary Kate McCoy. Wisconsin Public Radio. September 5, 2019. https://www.wpr.org/educator-theres-mass-teacher-exodus-not-shortage

Strauss, Valerie. "No Child Left Behind: What Standardized Test Scores Reveal About Its Legacy." *Washington Post* (March 10, 2015).

Turnbull, W. W. "Student Change, Program Change: Why SAT Scores Kept Falling." *College Board Report* 85, no. 2 (1985).

Vinson, Kathleen. "Hovering Too Close: The Ramifications of Helicopter Parenting in Higher Education." *Georgia State University of Law Review,* 29, no. 2 (2013): 424.

Vollmer, Jamie. *Schools Cannot Do It Alone.* New York: Enlightenment Press, 2010.

Yardley, Jonathan. "The High Cost of Grade Inflation." *Washington Post* (June 16, 1997).

About the Author

David C. Jeck is an award-winning educational leader currently serving in his fifteenth year as a Virginia public school superintendent. A former high school teacher, coach, and principal, Dr. Jeck has demonstrated courageous leadership at every turn, and he has championed a leadership philosophy that always puts children first.